Earth: Astrology's Missing Planet

In this very readable book, Chriss concept which should revolutioniz She blends her extensive experi metaphysical understanding, which combine together with clarity and perception. For those seeking the next step in astrology's unfolding journey, this is the book for you.
Richard Lawrence, international best-selling author and spiritual teacher

Earth: Astrology's Missing Planet is a wise and welcoming invitation to explore our relationship to the earth, a fundamental influence on our lives. Chrissie Blaze opens our eyes to the preciousness of our home planet, which is easily overlooked both in astrology and in life. This book explores how our wellbeing relies on our deep connection to the earth. It uncovers how each of us can fully express our unique talents and abilities by embracing and understanding the earth's influence on us.
Dr Jen Green ND, FABNO

Astrologers use our position on Earth as the point of reference for finding meaning in the planets above—yet while we are gazing outward at the sky, how easy it can be to overlook the planet on which we stand! Chrissie Blaze offers a thoughtful meditation on the planet we call home and Her powerful contributions to our astrological understanding.
Alia Wesala, LMSW, Consulting Astrologer

Earth: Astrology's Missing Planet takes astrology to a new level of awareness and transforms it into a more elegant and precise tool for the spiritual worker.

Brian Keneipp, author *Operation Earth Light*; Spiritual teacher

In true style of her namesake "Blaze" Chrissie Blazes new work *Earth: Astrology's Missing Planet: Reconnecting with Her Sacred Power* is blazing a homecoming for humanity's soul to reawaken and return to innocence in the garden of our Mother Planet, i.e. Mother Earth. Echoing the sacred feminine teachings of indigenous peoples the world over, Blaze's work realigns astrology to the original root knowledge, power and ancient wisdom of Mother Earth who holds each of us in our learnings in this lifetime. Linking us back to the superpower of Planet Earth and our own untapped collective feminine voice is not only timely, but truly urgent for humanity's conscious evolution. As Chrissie helps us reclaim the missing planet of Earth, she gives us the key to come home to ourselves and reclaim the kind of creative and transformational mother love that has the true power to reconnect and unite us as a global family and open the door to a future of personal and planetary peace.

White Eagle Medicine Woman/ Suraj Holzwarth, International Healer and Teacher, Author, Poet, Musician & Artist
Founder and Director: Grandmother Drum International Peace Project

Like the Parable of the Prodigal Son, Astrology has traced the HIStory of the Sun only to become destitute. Finally in *Earth: Astrology's Missing Planet*, Chrissie Blaze brings us home to our Divine Mother Earth and HERstory of immense love that offers great Spiritual progress. A must read for all spiritual seekers, let the healing begin!

Penny Golden, Founder Body Mind Spirit Radio Network & Body Mind Spirit Guide

Earth: Astrology's Missing Planet is a masterly and cogent blend of science and spirituality, to help us reconnect with our beautiful, living, breathing planetary home. Chrissie's book is a must-read for all astrologers, environmentalists, spiritual seekers and humanitarians, as we enter the brave new world of Aquarius.
Mollie Eilean Entwisle, M.Ed., ITEC, Teacher, writer, broadcaster on Numerology; author of *The Mystic Power of Numbers*

Chrissie Blaze's take on astrology is revolutionary. In her research, she fills in the long missing blanks and gracefully weaves spirituality with historic facts. This tapestry is unique and urgently needed in a time of radical changes on earth. Changes that we as a human race often cannot comprehend unless we re-align to our sacred mother planet. The earth does not need to change. We do. This book is a masterpiece on our truly needed growth from an astrological perspective.
Michaela Ashaneya Baumgartner, International Healer, Teacher and Performance Artist, The Whirling Rainbow Foundation

Earth: Astrology's Missing Planet

Reconnecting with Her Sacred Power

Earth: Astrology's Missing Planet

Reconnecting with Her Sacred Power

Chrissie Blaze

Winchester, UK
Washington, USA

First published by Dodona Books, 2018
Dodona Books is an imprint of John Hunt Publishing Ltd., Laurel House, Station Approach,
Alresford, Hants, SO24 9JH, UK
office1@jhpbooks.net
www.johnhuntpublishing.com
www.dodona-books.com

For distributor details and how to order please visit the 'Ordering' section on our website.

ISBN: 978 1 78535 662 9
978 1 78535 663 6 (ebook)
Library of Congress Control Number: 2017930557

A CIP catalogue record for this book is available from the British Library.

Design: Stuart Davies

Printed and bound by CPI Group (UK) Ltd, Croydon, CR0 4YY, UK

We operate a distinctive and ethical publishing philosophy in all
areas of our business, from our global network of authors to
production and worldwide distribution.

CONTENTS

Chrissie Blaze's Books

Workout for the Soul: Eight Steps to Inner Fitness, AsLan Publishing, Inc., November, 2001.

The Baby's Astrologer: Your Guide to Better Parenting Is In the Stars, Warner Books, 2003 (out of print).

Das Baby-Horoskop, Die besten Erziehungstipps stehen in den Sternen (Broschiert) Ullstein Tb; Auflage: 1 (Dez. 2004).

Bebek Astrolojisi, Hasan Oztoprah, Istanbul, 2004.

Power Prayer: A Program for Unlocking Your Spiritual Strength, Adams Media, 2003 (co-author, Gary Blaze; Foreword by Marianne Williamson).

How to Read Your Horoscope in 5 Easy Steps: How to Stop Reading Books (Except this One) and Start Reading Charts, O-Books, 2008.

Mercury Retrograde: Your Survival Guide to Astrology's Most Precarious Time of Year, O Books, 2008.

Baby Star Signs: Your Guide to Good Parenting Is In the Stars, O-Books, 2008.

Superstar Signs: Sun Signs of Heroes, Celebrities and You, O-Books, 2008.

Deeper Into Love: 7 Keys to a Heart-Based Spirituality, Mill City Press, 2010. Also E-book, 2011.

Karmic Astrology: Understanding the Keys to Your Soul's Purpose, E-book, 2011.

Power Prayer: A Program for Unlocking Your Spiritual Strength, Createspace 2012 (co-author, Gary Blaze; Foreword by Marianne Williamson); revised and expanded edition. Also E-Book 2012.

Healing Meditations: Blessings for the Heart, Createspace, 2013.

Healing Prayers: Blessings from the Heart, Createspace, 2013.

Soul Fitness: A 5-Step Plan for Inner and Outer Peace, Createspace, 2014. (Foreword by Dave Davies, The Kinks).

Acknowledgements

I thank The Master Dwal Khul as channeled by Alice Bailey in the book *Esoteric Astrology* for urging me and all astrologers to take into account in their astrological work the Earth upon which we reside. I am grateful to Dr. George King who taught the truth about the Earth and whose teachings inspired me to write this book.

Introduction

"We are spinning, spinning
Out of control
The rain dances cease
and the drought comes
The devas of storm
Bring flood
And we curse.
Cut off from Divine Mother
We are spinning, spinning
Out of control."
—Native American Guide

There is an awakening now taking place on Planet Earth. An evolutionary current sweeping through the hearts and minds of many, just as we face the threat of total annihilation. Chaos, terror, and ecological footprint breakdown coexists harshly with the gradual shift towards the desire for Oneness, peace, and integration of the burgeoning "New Age" movement.

Time, that measurement of change, is speeding up and, as a result, we feel pressure. Whether this becomes the pressure to change, evolve, and to embrace new ways of thinking and feeling, or the pressure that causes us to implode, is up to us. We are now witnessing both ends of the spectrum on planet Earth, and there's really only one choice. The winning side is, and always has been, the side that creates harmony and peace, love, healing, and selfless service. The long-term losers are those who, using their God-given freewill choose chaos, erroneously believing that this will take them Heavenwards or, just because they *can* choose chaos.

Every act we perform—good, bad, and indifferent—defines our future. An act of terrorism or mass murder will take the perpetrator down into the depths of their own hell, life after life, until at some point in the dim and distant future, the lesson of love—the intrinsic nature of us all—is learned.

The questions we may ask are, "*Do we have enough time left on the beautiful planet we are destroying for us to find harmony amidst the chaos? What can we do to change? What can we do to help?*"

A study of the enduring Spiritual truths, way above the limitations of religious dogma, will help us to find our way forward. Astrology too can also guide us and offer us a mirror by which we can, in a detached way, see ourselves authentically and see the way forward that we should take.

In this book, we shall see the vitally important influence of the Earth on our lives. Astrologically, we can see where this planet is in our horoscopes and what this means for us. By reconnecting with Earth's power, we can help ourselves to find harmony and sanity amidst the chaos and transform our way of thinking. We can heal ourselves through touching the sacred body of Mother Earth.

This vital connection to the Earth has gradually diminished over the past 500 years and our 'disconnect' has become increasingly intense in our modern era. The mechanistic approach in astrology and other disciplines that have been forged has been a factor in our increasing separation from the Earth. Now in this time of change and transformation, many preconceptions of the past have blown away to reveal the essential symbiotic relationship between humanity and Mother Earth. It is this relationship, if understood and nurtured, that will sustain us in the future and re-establish our right relationship with Mother Earth.

Earth: Astrology's Missing Planet shows the essential element missing from astrology books and teachings—the influence of the planet upon which we live, upon our lives and destiny.

As we look back over the changing role of astrology referred to in the ensuing chapters, we shall see a pattern emerging. The pendulum of history has swung from awakening to darkening and now has entered a transformative phase. This book will show how we can use the knowledge about the Earth to help transform our personal and global interrelationship with Mother Earth.

SECTION I

THE EARTH'S INFLUENCE IN ASTROLOGY

Chapter 1

Astrology's Missing Planet

"Forget not that the Earth delights to feel your bare feet, and the winds long to play with your hair."
—Kahlil Gibran

An important change that is now taking place is a greater urge towards an all-encompassing spirituality: one that is not necessarily related to a particular religion but is a worldview of Oneness and Truth. The seeds for this spiritual renaissance also began at the waning of the last Age and the waxing of this current Age.

Luminaries such as Madame Blavatsky and Alice Bailey were born at the close of the 19th Century, bringing the light of truth through Theosophical principles and esoteric works. This book on *Earth: Astrology's Missing Planet* was inspired in part by the teachings of The Ascended Master Dwal Kuhl (known as The Master DK) given through his telepathic contact with Alice Bailey and published in *Esoteric Astrology*, Lucis Publishing Company, New York, 1951. This book, together with a library of Alice Bailey's published works, was left to me by my beloved grandmother when she died; I was only four years of age at the time, but they became invaluable guidebooks for me in my teenage years and beyond.

Because of my burgeoning fascination with astrology, I was particularly interested in Alice Bailey's book *Esoteric Astrology* and over the years have read it on and off many times. Alice Bailey was a theosophist and a fascinating woman. She wrote twenty-six books in her lifetime and claims that twenty of these were dictated to her by the Ascended Master, Djwal Khul, known as *The Master DK*.

In *Esoteric Astrology*, The Master DK said one thing that I must have read dozens of times, but it wasn't until the middle of a powerful planetary configuration of revelation just around my birthday in April 2014 that it dawned on me—this was the time for me to write about an important truth contained in this esoteric work. Now was the time! I would do everything I could to bring it to the attention of not just the astrological community but also to the public.

The Master DK said:

There is one aspect of energy for which the modern astrologer makes very little allowance, and yet it is of paramount importance. This is the energy which emanates from or radiates from the Earth itself...astrologers have always emphasized the incoming influences and energies as they beat upon and play through our little planet, but they have omitted to take into adequate consideration the emanating qualities and forces which are the contribution of our Earth...to the larger whole.

In *Esoteric Astrology*, The Master Dwal Kuhl refers to The Earth as a non-sacred planet. I believe, however, that from a great Initiation of the Earth that took place on July 8, 1964 and which you can read about in the Resources section, the Earth is indeed a sacred planet. This means that Her light, Her bounty, and Her love are even more powerful, affecting us all. The responsibility for us is to acknowledge and accept Her great love and bounty, and then do all we can do to return it through our prayers, gratitude, and positive actions for Mother Earth.

Over the years, I have also had access to the advanced teachings of Dr. George King. As a close student of his, I learned first-hand from him that the Mother Earth is the most important aspect of any Spiritual philosophy.

I suddenly realized in a flash of illumination that this was the missing link in astrology I had been seeking for decades. I have studied, practiced, and taught astrology. I know I have helped many people and have received heart-warming testimonials to this effect from people all over the world. I have written astrology books to help demystify astrology's jargon so that anyone can understand and use it as a helpful tool.

However, I always felt deep down inside me that I was missing something very important. This revelation is the heart and soul of *Earth: Astrology's Missing Planet*. Just as mechanistic science removed the heart and soul from our worldview, many astrologers like myself (by refusing to acknowledge the Earth), had in effect missed an essential part of the ongoing puzzle that is astrology.

I believe it is long overdue for all astrologers and thinkers to question, understand, and appreciate the role of The Earth in our horoscopes. Any system concerned with evolution such as astrology, and indeed any spiritual philosophy or religion, must now take into account the Earth on which we live, move, and have our being. An understanding of our relationship to the Earth is even more essential at this pivotal time in our history than ever it was.

Most of us are now painfully aware that we are at the mercy of the Earth. There are earthquakes, volcanic eruptions, extreme weather conditions, and natural disasters of every kind. Indigenous cultures tell us that we are out of attunement to the Earth, and it is increasingly obvious that we are.

The Stairway between Heaven and Earth

In early civilizations there was a stairway between Earth and heaven, between the visible and invisible dimensions of life. Everything was intertwined and interrelated; the Cosmos was alive. The Earth was a Goddess and we all participated in a cosmic mystery in which the divine was woven like a golden thread in our lives. Dreams and visions were accepted as signs, voices of the soul guiding us onwards and upwards in our evolution. The subtle realms were as real as this physical realm, and our natural way was to align life with the greater life of the cosmos around us.

The science and intuitive art of astrology can play its part in helping to rebuild the stairway between heaven and Earth. We shall also examine the role of the Earth in our horoscope, what it means for us, and how to use this knowledge to re-establish a right relationship with our divine Mother Earth.

This is the major challenge facing us today. We need to become better stewards of Planet Earth first and foremost in our lives. It is only then that we can strive for a true universal fellowship. The time is short and there is much to be done; but, as quantum field theorists will tell you, a thought can change the world. However, as a metaphysician will tell you thought— when put into action—has a far greater power!

It is not too late for humanity to change the world for the better but first we must look at how this great disconnect from the Earth took place, and the ramifications it has had for us all.

Chapter 2

The Great Disconnect

"If you could see the Earth illuminated when you were in a place as dark as night, it would look to you more splendid than the moon."
—Galileo Galilei, Dialogue Concerning the Two Chief World Systems, 1632

"Once a photograph of the Earth, taken from the outside, is available, a new idea as powerful as any in history will be let loose."
—Attributed to Sir Fred Hoyle, 1948

"It's tiny out there.... It's ironic that we had come to study the Moon and it was really discovering the Earth."
—Bill Anders, Apollo 8, quoted in the 2008 Discovery TV series *When We Left Earth*

The Renaissance

Civilization moves forward extremely slowly and inexorably on this planet. We only have to look back over the past few hundred years to see that out of the bloodshed, violence, and chaos, humanity has simultaneously made phenomenal advances especially in the areas of science and technology. At the end of the dark period of prejudice and fear known as *The Middle Ages*, science began to rule supreme as erudite scientists poured over dusty tomes and telescopes. They brought the light and knowledge of the heavenly spheres to Earth, often in a blaze of controversy. This period was known as *The Renaissance*: a movement in Europe that inspired men to emerge once again into the light. There was an awakening of the mind and a thirst for knowledge so necessary after the shackles and restraints of the previous Centuries.

Renaissance mathematicians, scholars, and astronomers struggled to bring the world out of the darkness of The Middle Ages into the light of true scientific discovery. Astronomy at that time was not the modern observational science it is today but consisted of mathematical courses that enabled students to master many practical things, such as maritime navigation, as well as the casting of personal horoscopes.

Famous Astronomer-Astrologers

At that time, famous astronomers such as Copernicus, Kepler, and Galileo were also horoscope-casting astrologers. Since then, however, there has been a split between these twin studies of astronomy and astrology—two sides of the same coin.

Nicolas Copernicus died more than 450 years ago. He is still regarded as the father of modern astronomy who concluded that the Earth and all the other planets in this solar system revolved around the Sun. This revolution in the current worldview was brought about through the brilliance of this scientist/astrologer.

Later, another scientist who changed the course of history, Galilei Galileo (1564–1642), took up the baton of knowledge that was passed to Copernicus by the ancient Greeks. He too was an astronomer and astrologer, famous for his ability in the art of astrology, and many distinguished people of the time consulted with him.

A contemporary of Galileo, Johannes Kepler (1571–1630), was also an astrologer, astronomer, and mathematician who earned his living reading horoscopes for the rich and powerful. He wrote in *Harmonics Mundi* that *"The soul of the newly born baby is marked for life by the pattern of the stars at the moment it comes into the world, unconsciously remembers it, and remains sensitive to the return of configurations of a similar kind."* This is the basis of astrology today. Kepler is better known, however, for his laws of planetary motion and was also a key figure in the 17th Century's scientific revolution.

Although many people find it hard to take astrology seriously, they can easily take seriously its counterpart—astronomy. *Astronomy* means *'naming the stars'* and *astrology 'the logic of the stars.'* Astronomy represents the glove, while astrology is the living spirit of the hand inside the glove. It is strange that our analytical left-brain schools and universities teach us to make sense of the glove, while neglecting the thing that moves the hand inside. I feel sure it will not be too long, however, before these twin sciences can once again join hands, so to speak.

The Founding of Modern Science

The 17th Century was a pivotal period for science when the founders of modern science were born. These included Bacon, Descartes, and Newton. With Newtonian physics, science became mechanistic. Researchers discovered that many aspects of reality could be broken down into parts and put together again to see how they worked. It was believed that all matter in the universe could be reduced to the minutest particles, each separate and independent of each other, and devoid of any life.

This approach in physics was so successful that it was soon applied to our reality as a whole. This mechanistic approach is still held in high esteem even today, and is at the heart of materialism. It was determined that all events are determined by previously existing causes with no element of free will being possible, no evolution nor any intervention by a higher source.

This approach also undercut the foundations of astrology: the relationship between the heavens and humanity. The essential understanding of our relationship to the planets and stars, and especially to the Earth upon which we live, began to wane. According to this mechanistic view of science, the Earth was no longer relevant to humanity. She was no longer regarded as sacred but rather as a massive resource for our selfish and greedy needs.

Gradually and unerringly, the worldview changed. The

heavens above us became irrelevant. The magic and mystery of life was unerringly dimmed, and the importance of astrology along with it, except as a form of fortune telling. This was all part of a much larger split—our almost complete separation from The Mother Earth and Nature that actually began thousands of years ago and has continued in various forms until today.

In the midst of this harsh period, brilliant poets, authors, artists, and mystics strove to bring life and heart into the harshness of this new reality. Through their poetry and inspired writing, we could once again glimpse our true relationship with Mother Earth, long forgotten by the march of cold science.

William Blake (1757–1827), perhaps the most spiritual and mystical of English poets, urged us to look through the eyes of our soul. He reminded us:

To see a world in a grain of sand
And heaven in a wild flower
Hold infinity in the palm of your hand
And eternity in an hour.

Our Society Today

As one consequence of this split, man's ego reigned supreme. We began to believe that we could achieve our dreams no matter how they affected those around us; we became separated from the world around us and from God. This worldview has continued with ever-increasing materialism.

No longer is our desire for wealth and accumulation of possessions driven by hardship as it may have been in the past, but we have been brainwashed to believe through constant advertising that we can buy our way to fulfillment. We have witnessed over the past few decades many tragic suicides of the rich and famous who seem to have everything, and yet psycho-logical studies show there is no correlation between wealth and happiness.

We are somehow convinced that possessing as much as we possibly can during our lifetimes is a natural thing. However, if we take the time to think deeply, we shall see that this so-called 'natural' desire on our part is in fact destroying the environment, creating more poverty, speeding up global warming that is causing climate patterns to change, and many other negative conditions.

We live in this constant state of dissatisfaction with what we have and a desire to acquire more and more because there is an inner discontent, a lack of faith, a sense of separateness from the world around us and, especially, from Mother Earth. No matter how much we get, it never seems to be enough.

I am not saying that abundance isn't our birthright, and I certainly don't believe anyone should have to struggle through existence. I am referring to the materialistic madness where billionaires are increasing and reached an all-time high in 2014, while we still have starvation even in this, the richest country in the world, the USA. It is the type of materialistic madness where selfishness reigns supreme. I have known extremely wealthy people whose lives are devoted to taking care of the poor and sharing their wealth, and it is not this to which I am referring. These are wonderful people who understand that money is power, and this brings responsibility. They use this power to help, to heal, to serve; and there can be no higher or better use of wealth than this. I am talking about the type of senseless, selfish approach to wealth that drives people to distraction.

All this points to the fact that we—members of the human race—are out of balance. As a race, we have drawn further away from the concept of sacredness and transcendence that imbued the ancient civilizations. Now, for the most part, we live in a profane world experienced only through the five senses, where acquisitiveness seems to be, for many the *raison d'etre*, why we are here on Earth.

Even fascinating and important topics such as UFOs and Extraterrestrial intelligences have not captured the imagination and transformed the worldview of a people conditioned towards apathy by the lure of increasing materialism. This, despite the fact that many world leaders, scientists and astronauts, as well as ordinary people throughout the world, have seen Flying Saucers, believe in them and are sure they come from beyond this Earth. Even the incredibly intricate and beautiful crop circles, so prevalent in my own birth country of England, have failed to move the majority of people from their entrenched materialistic worldview.

Not surprisingly, at the same time as this rending of science and spirit, humanity, once so closely entwined with the Earth, is now conditioned to regard her as an abundant source of food, water, and energy. Materialism had virtually given us permission to take from her without any thought, without appreciation or gratitude for her bounty, and without concern for our future on this beautiful planet.

A New Era of Change—The Aquarian Age

A primary effect of this mechanistic view of science, combined with a burgeoning materialism, has been to render subjects like astrology, mysticism, spirituality, and poetry as irrelevant. The hopeful news is that in this present Aquarian Age this split is now gradually and unerringly being recognized and repaired by the very science that disregarded it in the first place.

The Astrological Ages represent changes of consciousness; and each lasts approximately 2,160 years, as one-twelfth (1/12) of a larger measurement of time known as *The Great Year*. The previous Age was Pisces and this current Age of Aquarius is now dawning.

Over 2,000 years ago, before the beginning of the last Age of Pisces, the seeds of global selfishness had flourished into a dangerous, destructive pattern, witnessed too often upon this

Earth. As has happened throughout our long history, the Ancient Ones took pity upon our plight; and the great Cosmic Avatar of Love, The Master Jesus, was born into the lifecycle of Earth. He came, as have other great Avatars before Him, to sacrifice Himself in order to *buy us time* so that we could once again return to the Laws of God.

The Master Jesus demonstrated lessons associated with the zodiac sign of Pisces, namely—love, sacrifice, and service. According to Luke 22:10 and Mark 14:13, Jesus said, *"A man will meet you carrying an earthen pitcher of water; follow him into the house where he goes in."*

Some astrologers interpret this to mean that Jesus was announcing the coming Age of Aquarius because Aquarius is represented by the water bearer carrying a pitcher of water. This is symbolic of the waters of truth being poured to everyone as *"power to the people."* The availability of astrology to everyone through computers is one aspect of this power.

When we move from one astrological Age to another, the mass consciousness of humanity is subjected to different influences, which help to bring about a collective change. Some of the positive aspects associated with this New Age include a more a global humanitarian approach and a new blending of science and spirituality.

We are now on the cusp of this Age, and the changeover from one set of influences to another can take several hundred years, bringing a time of global chaos but also great potential: scientific revolution as well as revelation. At this pivotal time in our history, we are experiencing within ourselves and seeing in the world around us, an urge to break away from previous limitations, seeking a new level of freedom.

One aspect of this freedom is that, unlike the scientist/astronomers of the past, now almost anyone can sit in their local coffee shop and calculate a horoscope. Astrology, like science or medicine, is evolving. Quantum field theorists, who deal with the smallest subatomic particles of matter, have proven what metaphysicians have always taught—that consciousness affects matter. In other words, our environment is no longer a static thing that defines us, as we have been led to believe, but *we* constantly affect and change *it*.

The astrologer for this Age, as well as being thoroughly trained in the discipline of astrology, should therefore also be heart-based and intuitive with a loving intent. Now, this once fatalistic study must move with the flow of evolution—Godwards. A spiritual, evolutionary, and soul-centered approach is now required. This new approach to astrology is variously called *esoteric astrology, evolutionary astrology, soul-centered astrology, karmic astrology,* and *spiritual astrology.*

For the purposes of this book, I use the term *spiritual astrology* because I believe that spirituality is the quality most needed on Earth at this time. Spirituality is not tied to a particular religious organization, but is the approach to life of the person dedicated to the expression of soul-based values rather than purely materialistic ones.

A spiritual person is one who is impressed to help others, putting his beliefs into action through selfless service. This is the so-called ordinary man and woman who can do extraordinary things through their loving actions for those they have never met. It may be the rescue worker who digs through dangerous rubble to save a life; a person who raises her hands and heart in prayer; or someone who rescues animals or helps the environment in some way. There are many ways to serve and live a spiritual life in these pivotal days of change.

Spiritual astrology, like quantum physics, teaches how we can affect the world around us. It shows us how we can become masters of our fate rather than subject to it. The constant change expressed in quantum physics is also revealed through spiritual astrology. At the heart of spiritual astrology is, I believe, the beautiful Earth upon which we live, move, and evolve.

Earth: Astrology's Missing Planet, will shed some light on this influence; but more importantly, it will show how we can use this knowledge to become Her loving children rather than mindless parasites.

Chapter 3

Astrology, New Science, and the Aquarian Age

"Until a man duplicates a blade of grass, Nature can laugh at his so-called scientific knowledge. Remedies from chemicals will never stand in favorable comparison with the products of Nature, the living cell of a plant, the final result of the rays of the Sun, the mother of all life."
—Thomas Edison

It is always a wonderful thing when science proves what the ancient occultists or indigenous cultures have known all along. This coming together of science and spirituality will take place more and more frequently, as this is an inherent part of the New Age in which we live—the Aquarian Age.

For many centuries, the wise ones have known that Mother Earth is a living Intelligence, highly evolved and more alive than any of us. James Lovelock published his book *The Gaia Hypothesis* in 1979 in which he proposed the idea that the Earth is a single living Entity. The 18th Century "father of geology," James Hutton, described the Earth as a type of super-organism.

John Nelson in his book, *The Breathing Earth*, was able to put together a year's worth of the seasonal transformations of the Earth and what these look like from Outer Space. Once these are arranged in a sequence, one can see the Earth's in and out movement, as if She is breathing.

In 2008, *www.space.com* published a news item that said, *"Earth's atmosphere was known to breathe in a cycle lasting nearly a month."* Now, scientists say the planet takes a quick breath every few days, which was unexpected.

All of these findings and more have brought a growing

awareness of the interconnectedness of everything on planet Earth, as well as the impact that we humans have on Earth's processes. We can no longer think of ourselves as separate, for everything we do affects the Earth—good, bad, and indifferent. Another truth is that, while the Earth can easily live without humanity, humanity cannot live without Her, and so it behooves us to take *very seriously* this disconnect to our planetary home and do everything in our power, both individually and collectively, to rectify it.

James Lovelock believes that it is now too late. I believe, however, that if we, as a critical mass of caring humans, were to make the changes suggested in this book and others, and not wait for the politicians to lead the way, we can save our future on planet Earth.

The Earth's Heartbeat

It was in 1953 that Professor W.O. Schumann of the University of Munich first discovered that the Earth produces very specific vibrational pulsations. A year later, Dr. Schumann, together with Dr. Herbert Konig, who was to become his successor, confirmed that this frequency was 7.83 Hz, and years later this frequency came to be known as the "Schumann Resonance," otherwise called "the Earth's heartbeat."

We are actually living on a planet that constantly emits the frequency and energy of Love.

However, modern research indicates that, because trillions of watts of microwave energy has been pumped into the ionosphere, this is boosting the average frequency of the Schumann resonance even higher.[1]

This fascinating research about the Schumann Resonance also led to the finding that there was a correlation between the Earth's heartbeat and the brain rhythms of humans, and this has been studied by researchers throughout the world.

Dr. Wolfgang Ludwig researched the Schumann Resonance

and the connection between humans and Mother Earth for many years to find what frequencies are present in a healthy environment. Part of his research involved the ancient Chinese teachings of Yin (the feminine Earth energy from below) and Yang (the masculine Sun energy from above). The Chinese teachings state that both Yin and Yang should be in balance for good health, and Dr. Ludwig's research confirmed this ancient teaching.

Another researcher, Professor R. Wever from the Max Planck Institute, built an underground bunker which completely blocked out magnetic fields, including the "heartbeat" frequency of 7.83 Hz. Young, healthy volunteers lived there for four weeks and, during this time, they all suffered from migraines and emotional distress. All the volunteers were young and healthy so there were no major health breakdowns as there could have been with older or sicker people. They were then given a brief exposure to the 7.83 Hz frequency and their health stabilized, proving the importance of being in harmony with the Earth that we now take for granted.

Michael Hutchison states in his book *Mega Brain Power* that the 7.83 Hz frequency appears to have a wide range of beneficial effects on human beings ranging from reports of enhanced healing to accelerated learning. When a biological system vibrates at this frequency, it can be said to be in a state of resonance or attunement with the planet's own magnetic frequency.

Research shows what the indigenous cultures and wise ones have always known—that we are naturally attuned to the heartbeat of the Earth—and it is not by chance that She is regarded as our Divine Mother.

Unfortunately, many experts believe that all the man-made electromagnetic field (EMF) frequencies from computers, cell phones, TVs, power lines, microwaves, radio waves, and so forth, interrupt links with the Schumann Resonance, and mask the benefits, causing stress, migraines, insomnia, and other far more serious conditions that can take years to come to light. This is yet another form of pollution on our planet.

Unfortunately this pollution is not going away as it is now part of the world in which we live. Therefore, it is now more important than ever to find ways to restore our harmony with Mother Earth.

The physical condition of early astronauts deteriorated severely whilst in outer space, away from the Schumann Resonance. According to www.earthpulse.net, the Russian Space Agency discovered that, by placing Schumann wave generators in spacecraft that mimicked the Earth's frequency, the health and wellbeing of astronauts improved, especially their bone density. NASA then included these Schumann generators in the Space Station. This once again proved that we cannot be completely healthy when we are disconnected from this natural frequency, and so achieving this is an important foundation for good health.

How Astrology Can Help

An important advance since I constructed my first real astrology chart using logarithms in the 1970s is that now the majority of people in the Western world have access to astrology. If they wish to, they can now construct a chart within seconds using simple astrology software on their computers or cell phones. Astrology is no longer a complex study reserved for the few. Today, thanks to the personal computer revolution, this helpful, liberating study of you and me is now freely available.

This new accessibility of astrology is one example of the unveiling of "the Mysteries," a hallmark of this Aquarian Age. This current accessibility, combined with a deeper understanding of "astrology's missing planet, The Earth," can play a significant part in helping to rebuild the connection that once existed between us, The Earth, and the Cosmos.

Everything is Alive

To really understand this real and vital connection, we first have to understand that everything is alive. There is a tendency to think that we humans, together with the animal kingdom, are the only living beings on Earth. When we think deeper, we would include Nature in all its glory. Deeper still, we would include the kingdom of the devas and nature spirits, the Sun, the Moon, and the glorious living planets. However, the most advanced life form that we touch every day of our lives is the very Earth beneath our feet.

Quantum field theorists explain that everything is energy, and everything is alive and in a state of constant change. Since we are bundles of energy (solidified Sunlight) and microcosms of the Universe, cosmic energy patterns affect us. Astrology is the study of the influence of these cosmic energies on our affairs and behavior. Astrology too is evolving and gaining more relevance in this new age of science.

I believe that this shift from mechanistic thinking to a growing awareness that everything *is alive* is one of the most important changes of this Age. Not that this is new. Over 2,000 years ago, Plato described the Universe as *"a single living Creature that encompasses all of the living creatures that are within it."* However, what *is* new today is that this viewpoint is now becoming acceptable to both modern science and spiritual traditions. This is an important shift in consciousness towards Truth and Oneness.

This view overcomes the profound separation that has erroneously existed between us and all around us. It was less than a hundred years ago that Einstein, while developing his theory of relativity, still considered the universe as a static, unchanging system.

The implications for a living, expanding universe that contains hundreds of billions of stars are enormous, particularly so for Astrology, the study of the influence of the planetary bodies and cosmic energies on our affairs and behavior. As a result, astrology too is evolving and gaining more relevance today.

Another significant breakthrough in science is the understanding of non-locality. Previously, galaxies beyond ours appeared so remote that they were regarded as separate from ours. Now, experiments have shown that things that seem to be separate are really connected in ways that transcend ordinary time and space. Physicist David Bohm says that the entire Universe—or the whole of God's Creation—is one *"single, undivided whole."* This is a fundamental teaching of mystics and metaphysicians.

Dr. George King taught many years ago that even a rock is alive and has feeling. He also taught over sixty years ago that the Earth was a living Intelligence, far more evolved than humanity as a whole.[2]

This concept of the Earth as an advanced, living, breathing Intelligence is at the heart of this book. The Goddess Terra—Mother Earth—She—is no longer a lump of lifeless rock, nor has She ever been. Now we can glimpse the truth that She is our Mother. We live, move, think, and have our being on Her body and within Her great aura, as one interconnected unit.

Although there is a growing awareness of Oneness brought about through quantum physics, as well as through the reaching out into the cosmos by the astronauts and later Hubble, and the birth of an ever-strengthening global evolutionary urge towards spirituality, there are still seeds of the former age, difficult to shake. We are still in materialism's grip. Even the spiritual movement is not for the faint-hearted and it takes all of our discernment to find the truth amongst the rubble of false teaching. Here many are still conditioned to believe that the way to our enlightenment is through expensive courses, or through slick teachers who claim to be "New Age" and yet focus on an unhealthy obsession with self.

However, as we move through and beyond this stage as we must, we shall then see *Oneness* not only as an agreeable concept, but as a living reality.

Inner Space and Outer Space

It was only relatively recently that humanity was able to experience the full beauty of Earth, thanks to the early astronauts. When I was young I was inspired, together with the rest of the world, with the excitement of the Space Missions and with what the astronauts shared after seeing Earth from space for the first time.

This planet is not terra firma. It is a delicate flower and it must be cared for. It's lonely. It's small. It's isolated, and there is no resupply. And we are mistreating it. Clearly, the highest loyalty we should have is not to our own country or our own religion or our hometown or even to ourselves. It should be to, number two, the family of man, and number one, the planet at large. This is our home, and this is all we've got.
—Scott Carpenter, Mercury 7 astronaut, speech at Millersville University, Pennsylvania. 15 October 1992

It truly is an oasis—and we don't take very good care of it. I think the elevation of that awareness is a real contribution to saving the Earth.
—Dave Scott, Apollo 9 and 15 astronaut, interview for 2007 movie *In the Shadow of the Moon.*

You develop an instant global consciousness, a people orientation, an intense dissatisfaction with the state of the world, and a compulsion to do something about it. From out there on the moon, international politics look so petty. You want to grab a politician by the scruff of the neck and drag him a quarter of a million miles out and say, 'Look at that, you son of a bitch.'
—Edgar Mitchell, Apollo 14 astronaut, *People* magazine, 8 April 1974.

One thing these early astronauts experienced when they saw Earth from space was a powerful sense of great beauty and fragility of planet Earth, and they understood how humanity's role was to care of Her.

This is the time to revisit this awe for Mother Earth. After all, She is still the same as She was in the 1960s, and She is actually even more advanced in Her evolution today. It is we who have stepped away from Her, and got caught up in what seems to be an ever-increasing madness of destruction.

My husband Gary and I were keynote speakers at the *Living the Field* Conferences in London over several years from 2003, and we had the honor to meet and dine with the group of cutting-edge scientists who were fellow conference speakers. These included the late astronaut Captain Edgar Mitchell. It was in 1971 that Dr. Mitchell and other crew members of Apollo 14, blasted off from Cape Kennedy bound for the Moon and you can see some of his reactions to his first trip to the Moon above.

Over lunch, Dr. Mitchell shared that he was a different, more enlightened man who landed in the Pacific just ten days after his take-off. This brilliant MIT/NASA-trained scientist had an epiphany. The experience he had in space changed him forever. He felt an overwhelming sense of connectedness or what he referred to as *"the ecstasy of unity."* In his words:

> *It occurred to me that the molecules of my body and the molecules of the spacecraft itself were manufactured long ago in the furnace of one of the ancient stars that burned in the heavens about me. And there was a sense that our presence as space travelers, and the existence of the universe itself, was not accidental, but that there was an intelligent process at work. I perceived the universe as in some way conscious.*

When he left NASA a year later, he founded The Institute of Noetic Science, the beginning of a new journey of exploration—

from outer space to the inner worlds. Since then, he dedicated the rest of his life to revealing the mysteries of consciousness, evolution, and spirituality.

The good news is that it does not require us to leave our planetary home to experience Oneness. Blissful and ecstatic states have been achieved throughout our history by men and women including Dr. George King with whom I worked closely for 25 years.

Dr. King was a visionary, ahead of his time, and his mission of planetary healing and enlightenment was to help ensure a future for humanity as well as to help the Earth. Dr. King talked about a need for change towards a spiritual consciousness in order to solve what he taught was the major energy crisis facing us. He called this *The Spiritual Energy Crisis*. He devoted his life to devising global healing missions to help bring more of this harmonious *spiritual energy* of Love into the world. These missions are continued today by the organization he founded, The Aetherius Society, of which I am active member.[3]

Dr. Edgar Mitchell also talks of the need to create a sustainable civilization: a *"shift in consciousness that starts to recognize we're all in this together, we're all part of the same mold."*

A Magical Universe

One doesn't need to be an astrologer to see that, despite the growing materialism and disconnect with Mother Earth, there is indeed a major global shift simultaneously taking place. Many people, entranced by politics or a desire for abundance that is just out of their reach, see a frightening and hopeless future. Others, aware of increasing feelings of fear and discontent, bury their heads in the sand. A relative few realize that the universe is magical, and even apparently impossible situations can shift.

As a child, you knew life was magical before you were conditioned to believe it was not. As a three-year-old, I frequently dived into the swimming pool and breathed underwater. I later learned that this was impossible. Personally, I espouse the *Alice in Wonderland* philosophy of believing six impossible things before breakfast. Why wouldn't I? I'm an astrologer, and despite what other astrologers may tell you, the whole basis of astrology rests on illusion. Paradoxically, though, it is also one of the purest studies of truth. Since it deals with the energies and forces of the cosmos, why should we expect to understand it by intellect alone?

Astrology is a study of something so much greater than we are, that it takes all of us—our intellect, our intuition, our inspiration—to begin to grasp it.

So, although astrology is as much a science as any, using it is definitely an intuitive art through which we can learn to interpret things essentially beyond our comprehension. I believe that a truly scientific view of the universe is one in which awe, wonder, and inspiration go hand in hand with observation and statistics. I am not alone in this belief. Albert Einstein summed it up when he said, *"The most beautiful and most profound experience is the sensation of the mystical. It is the sower of all true science."*

Chapter 4

The Planets in Astrology

"It suddenly struck me that that tiny pea, pretty and blue, was the Earth. I put up my thumb and shut one eye, and my thumb blotted out the planet Earth. I didn't feel like a giant. I felt very, very small."
—Neil Armstrong

To the modern, soul-centered astrologer, the planets are regarded as ancient, living intelligences within a living solar system, within a living galaxy. There are many theories about how astrology works, but I subscribe to the theory that everything is energy. We are bundles of solidified Sunlight; each planet radiates its own unique energies through the electromagnetic force fields existing between them. The relationships between the planets, known as *aspects*, reveal the working out of a Divine Plan in which we live, move, and have our being. The more we understand and align with this Cosmic Plan, the more of our Spiritual potential we unfold.

Although the following pages offer a breakdown of each planetary influence, one has to look at them all working together as a wonderful planetary symphony. We use the energies of the planets every day of our lives, and "color" these influences according to our own motives, karma, and evolutionary desires—or the opposite. However difficult and challenging certain astrological periods seem to be, my belief is that the planetary energies are always good—why? Because they are part of God's Plan for our evolution. Even the most difficult health period, for example, can teach us valuable lessons of strength and fortitude. The most challenging relationship issues can, if we are honest with ourselves, bring deeper understanding and love.

Astrologers have regarded the Moon, Mercury, Venus, and Mars as the "personal" or "inner" planets because they particularly affect each of us at a profoundly personal level. The slower-moving "outer planets" have more of a generational influence. The Sun is in a category of its own, as you will see below.

It is beneficial to understand the nature, position, and influence of each of the planets in your horoscope—including the long-forgotten planet Earth—as well as other significant points such as your Ascendant. Once we understand these energies, we can then use this power more positively and consciously in our lives.

The Sun

The Sun in your horoscope represents your character and one of the things we are here on Earth to develop. The astrological sign in which the Sun was when you were born is what your soul has chosen as a tool to help you through life.

The Sun is both the exoteric and the esoteric ruler of the sign of Leo. If you fully immerse yourself in your Sun energies, you will become the most creative, most joyful and effective loving human being. If you ignore it, as many people do, you will feel a vague sense of being lost, of not achieving what you are here to do. Your Sun sign represents your soul in spiritual astrology.

For example, you may be shy, reserved, and lacking in confidence, but born a Leo. You may shun astrology saying, *"I'm nothing like my Sun sign!"* My response is *"Well, you should be!"* Being born a Leo means you are here to learn to express the Leo qualities of confidence and leadership. An enlightened Leo identifies with the Soul as well as the personality. The result is an integration and fusion of these two to bring a wise, magnanimous, generous, and loving expression.

To bring a stronger relationship between your soul and your personality, we first should remind ourselves that we are divine spirit. Although we have a physical body, we are not that physical body, but it is a temple which our soul inhabits while we are alive on the physical plane. However, we also should remember that our life on this physical realm is vitally important.

We have emotions; sometimes these are strong and unruly. When we remember that we are not our emotions but allow our soul to guide us, we can begin to master our emotions and learn the path of true Love. We have a mind and thoughts that seem to lead us. However, when we remember to allow our soul to speak, we can then use our intelligence, discernment, and mind as tools.

This is a joyful journey of transformation and transmutation of our basic nature, not negation of the personality. Abundance on all levels is the natural order, but our obsessive attachment to abundance or its lack is unnatural and one of the causes of the problems on Earth.

Once we make a surrender *God-wards*, we will draw to ourselves a natural order that will bring signs, people, and teachings as guideposts along the way, moving us even further in this direction.

Life is about growth, evolution, and eventual enlightenment. Every person is here learning how to express talents and abilities, the seeds of which are shown in their horoscopes at the moment of their birth.

The Moon

While the Sun represents your character, born from decisions made, the Moon is your personality born from feelings, needs, habits, and patterns of early conditioning. The exoteric ruler of the Moon is the sign of Cancer; the esoteric ruler is Virgo.

The majority of humanity is more attuned to the Moon in their charts as there is an emphasis on personality. We can regard the Sun as our present and future, and the Moon as our past. Many of our habits no longer work for us as we move towards the light of the Sun. To the spiritually centered person, the Moon loses its grip, and she is no longer so attached to this emotional lunar energy. While the Sun is your adult, the Moon is your inner child.

While it is important to center in your Sun sign, you can't afford to ignore your Moon's needs. If you do, you will just keep pushing your feelings and insecurities "under the carpet," and for people not firmly anchored in a Spiritual philosophy, these will fester and ultimately build to a crisis point.

For example, if you have a Libran Moon, you have a strong innate sense of justice. When life all around you is unfair, you can choose to ignore the injustice and bury your head in the sand. However, if you do that long enough, it will backfire. Although, ultimately, we don't have power over others, we do have the power to change ourselves. If you see no justice, perhaps it is because you are supposed to be bringing justice. If you act in the light of this feeling, you are satisfying your Moon's needs and you will feel happier about yourself.

While the Sun acts, the Moon reacts. How do you instinctively react to problems? How do things make you feel? What do you need to be secure? The Moon infuses you with memories from the past, while the Sun reflects the here and now.

Mercury

Mercury is the messenger of the Gods and the alchemist, and as such plays an important position in our lives. Madame H.P. Blavatsky in *The Secret Doctrine*, said, *"Mercury is called the first of the celestial Gods, the God Hermes...to which God is attributed the invention of and the first initiation of men into Magic."*

Mercury represents Mind, which allows humanity to consciously bring through them energies of high intuition and inspiration from the higher mental realms. It is the esoteric ruler of the sign of Aries and the exoteric ruler of the signs of duality, Gemini and Virgo. It is the faculty of awareness and self-consciousness that separates us from the animal kingdom.

On the basic level, Mercury represents duality and all communication. It is the planet of day-to-day expression. *"What shall I buy at the store? What time is my appointment with the dentist? Should I cook my boyfriend dinner or wait for him to take me out?"*

Mercury does the talking and rules your thought processes. It is the light in your eye, your coordination, your intelligence and your ideas. It is unemotional and curious. The sign your Mercury is in and the aspects it makes to the other planets, shows how neat your handwriting is and what chance you have to become an author.

Our modern world is mercurial, as communication is speedy and instantaneous. The influence of Mercury is felt more than ever before, bringing people and countries together through global telephone networks and the Internet. People make connections through emails and find information instantly through Google. The Mercurial influence is friendly, but it doesn't make a deep connection. Think of the nature of emails, and you will understand the type of connection Mercury makes.

Venus

Esoterically, the planet Venus is the ruler of the sign of Gemini, and the spiritual aspect of Venus reveals that quality of consciousness of pure Love, which is the energy of preservation throughout Creation. This planet is about relationship, synthesis, and Oneness; and, on a higher level, represents the linking of the higher mind with the lower.

On an exoteric level, Venus is the ruler of both Taurus and Libra. Venus is that miracle-making part of your horoscope if you allow it to be. Like all the planets, you can choose to use its lower manifestation of the energy or its higher, more mystical, alchemical version.

Venus operates like a refined version of your Moon and it rules the arts. It represents two main areas of life: love, and our value systems. It affects how we handle the things we value which include money, possessions, photographs, paintings, music, friendships, or loved ones.

Venus rules your sentiments and ability to give and receive love, to appreciate and be appreciated. It is your charm factor (or not), your grace and beauty, the ability to get along with others in relationships and social graces. Where it is in your horoscope is your *Attraction Principle*, i.e., your ability to attract things and people and your artistic nature. Venus energy seeks harmony, and people with Venus prominent are often peacemakers. In Mahatma Gandhi's horoscope, his two most prominent planets were Uranus, the awakener, and Venus, the peacemaker. On the negative side, you can be self-indulgent, self-centered, vain, and superficial.

Mars

Mars is both the esoteric and exoteric ruler of Scorpio, and also the exoteric ruler of Aries. Both these signs of the zodiac are seen as strong and powerful in character, but Mars has a dual expression. On the one hand, as the ruler of Aries, we think of energy, action and desire; however, there is an also innate desire and understanding of the need for sacrifice. This can manifest as the sacrifice of the soldier in battle who will lay down his life for his brother, or the incarnating soul who willingly sacrifices the bliss of the higher mental realms in order to return to this physical plane so that he can give service to humanity.

With Scorpio, Mars brings about the tests and challenges that are an essential part of the growth of the spiritually motivated man. The battle of Mars is the battle between the lower self and the higher self until self-mastery is achieved.

On a basic level, Mars is the planet of energy, action, and desire. It represents action and is the way you assert yourself. It is what fires you up, what gets you out of bed in the morning, and what lights your fire. It is also your survival instinct. On a physical level, whereas Venus rules romantic attraction, Mars is associated with sexual attraction. Mars shows how you apply your drives, express your enthusiasm, and the types of experiences you seek.

People sometimes dismiss Martian types as being assertive and bloody-minded. You might not like those people who look you straight in the eye, daring you to mess with them, but you secretly have to respect their strength. Look at the power of Mars in your horoscope and you can see how likely you are to run into a burning building to save a stranger.

Never underestimate this planet. Without the power Mars, you would never get out of bed in the morning. It is a vital energy that drives you to build and to achieve your goals. Understand its power of raw energy, embrace it, wield it, and you too can conquer fear. Remember, bravery is the first freedom,[4] and the positive Mars energy is courageous, assertive, and directed. On the negative side, it is impulsive, rash, impatient, aggressive, and forceful.

Jupiter

As we enter the New Age, Jupiter's influence is an important one because it is the esoteric ruler of the sign of Aquarius. Jupiter is the planet of integration, bringing together the higher mind and the lower, the head and the heart, as well as diverse groups of people. It is the planet of wisdom and spiritual growth.

Exoterically, Jupiter rules the mutable signs of both Sagittarius and Pisces. It is known as the planet of expansion and abundance. Jupiter seeks insight through knowledge. Some of this planet's keywords include tolerance, morality, gratitude, hope, good will, honor, the law, religion, and philosophy. It is where we seek to be generous and also what we take for granted. Jupiter also represents the luck or good karma factor in your horoscope.

I recently received an email from a desperate family. An

elderly aunt, who knew a little about astrology, saw Jupiter transits in her chart and thought she was about to win the lottery. She was having a great time contacting scam merchants all over the world and spending a small fortune trying to make this happen! The lady was on a roll, thinking big in typical Jupiterean fashion; she was displaying some of Jupiter's influence on a basic level: an urge to overspend, and a certain blind optimism.

Jupiter also represents things that bring abundance, joy, and expansion, such as music, art, color, and sound. The more negative manifestations of Jupiter include excess and overindulgence.

Saturn

Saturn is the great teacher, the ruler of Capricorn and the co-ruler of Aquarius. This wonderful, yet serious planet of reality checks and boundaries is associated with restrictions and limitations. While Jupiter expands, Saturn constricts. Saturn brings structure and meaning to your world and if used wisely helps you to build your dreams on firm foundations. Saturn reminds you of responsibilities and brings definition. Saturn makes you aware of the need for self-control, maturity, and wisdom.

Why should a great teacher bring limitation? Allow me to explain how it works. If you act out of tune with the universal flow of life that is geared towards evolution and love, Saturn's energies will block you. If you go selfishly towards what you want, ignoring the needs of others, Saturn will eventually stop you. If your choices become purely self-centered based on what you *want* rather than what you really *need*, Saturn will limit your life in some way so that you wake up. This limitation can come through ill health, an authority figure or some external discipline. Saturn is the great Teacher, teaching us to operate from a less self-centered place.

Saturn is associated with authority figures and traditional values. In childhood, the discipline, rules, and regulations imposed by parents, teachers, and other authority figures were not always pleasant but they helped us to learn. Similarly, Saturn's energies help us to learn through discipline.

Uranus

The energies of Uranus are electric and crammed with change. Uranus is forward-looking, original, and rules the "genius" factor. It gives the ability to tap the higher intuition and aspects of mind. This unpredictable planet is the ruler of Aquarius, together with Saturn. Uranus is associated with technology, innovation, discovery, and all that is progressive. This Aquarian Age is ruled by both the tradition and discipline of Saturn and the progressiveness of Uranus.

A typical Uranian type of personality was Nikola Tesla who had Uranus rising when he was born within one degree of his Ascendant. Tesla invented the alternating-current induction motor, a device that was previously considered to be impossible to design. Until Tesla had decided to confront this supposedly unsolvable problem, direct current was considered to be the only way to distribute electricity. Tesla's invention revolutionized the modern use and distribution of electricity and enabled cities to receive a safe, reliable form of electrical current. This awesome feat was achieved on a large scale for the first time with his lighting of the 1893 Chicago World Columbian Exposition. Tesla was indeed a genius.

On the positive side, Uranus is associated with enlightenment, progressiveness, objectivity, and ingenuity. It's where we go against tradition or authority that is outworn and no longer serves the good of the whole. Uranus represents the spark of intuition that spurs invention or investigation. The negative expression of Uranus is a rebel without a cause and irresponsibility.

Neptune

Neptune is the planet of inspiration, dreams, psychic receptivity, illusion, and confusion. Neptune is the sensitive poet and mystic, and the ruler of Pisces.

The Neptune-ruled person strives for communion, the ecstasy of never having to leave her lover's or her mother's arms. At a higher level, it is the person who yearns for union with the Divine. The god, Neptune, rules the ocean and it is this type of an oceanic oneness, this blissful state that Neptunian-type personalities crave.

I have a prominent Neptune in my horoscope. My mother told me that when I went to the seaside as a small child I would wobble into the water in my romper suit and white sun hat and sit there motionless for hours at a time. I don't remember the experience in great detail, but I do remember how happy I felt. I was definitely a water-baby. I proudly told my frantic parents who had found me after being submerged in a swimming pool for several minutes that I had been breathing underwater. To this day, I'm sure I did. I can remember the feeling of oneness. I had a great love for water, and swimming was second-nature to me. Unfortunately, I contracted skin allergies due to chlorine and polluted seawater, and now my water exploits are few and far between. However, I later took up the other Neptunian pursuit of mysticism like a psychic duck to water.

Neptune is associated with intuition, subtlety, and spiritual enlightenment. It is the planet of mercy and compassion. The more negative manifestations of Neptune include deception, trickery, deceit, guilt, and addiction.

Pluto

I have a lot to say about Pluto, which was demoted from its lofty planetary status by the International Astronomical Union on the same day that an important 14-year cycle started—August 23, 2006. However, strangely enough as I write this on October 2, 2014, the latest news out today is that the Union's definitions of a planet had sparked many debates in the ensuing years. Then, the

Harvard Smithsonian Center for Astrophysics jumped into the debate and finally declared on September 18, 2014 that tiny Pluto is indeed a planet. It reached this conclusion by having some experts discuss the definition of a planet and then let the audience vote—and they voted correctly. Astrologers have had no doubt all along that the IAU was wrong.

Showing how out of tune the astronomers were, this day of Pluto's demotion was, astrologically speaking, an important turning point in Pluto's influence. It's a shame that astronomers and astrologers can't get along like they used to because they could help each other to understand the universe. I predict that astrology and astronomy will become twin sciences again as they used to be.

If you will excuse a bit of techno-speak, the 367-day cycles created by the orbits of Earth and Pluto around the Sun (called *Pluto's Synodic Cycles*) had been occurring in sidereal Scorpio for many years (1995–2006), but from August 23, 2006 now occur in sidereal Sagittarius until 2020. This important new cycle signifies a change in collective consciousness. What does this mean to us?

Pluto is now urging us to shift up a few levels to a greater truth of who we really are and to pursue our ideals more passionately. This marks the ending of a time when false beliefs prevailed and the beginning of a time when truth will win. This is, therefore, a vitally important phase.

It seemed so typical that, just as Pluto power was about to take us up to new heights, a group of astronomers tried to render it ineffective. The good news is that despite what labels are slapped on or taken off Pluto, they have absolutely no effect on its power. From July 2006 to 2020, Pluto will continue to clear away ignorance so that the light of truth can shine.

How does Pluto, the ruler of Scorpio, work in your horoscope? Its intense energies are transformative. It operates rather like an atom bomb that disturbs and brings things to the surface, or like a spotlight shining on our fears and urging us to face them honestly. Propaganda, falseness, hypocrisy, and weakness are not of Pluto's alchemical realm. Pluto's quest is to transmute the base metal of your lower nature into the gold of your higher nature through change.

Where you find Pluto in your horoscope is where you find endings and new beginnings, spiritual growth, and rebirth. When you come through a Pluto transit, you are changed forever but, during the process, you probably don't realize what's going on. If you refuse to accept your deepest soul needs to change, you will have it painfully thrust upon you. There is actually nothing to fear; you just have to surrender to the mysterious process of this complete transformation. Just think of the butterfly's painful emergence from the chrysalis. That is what is happening in human terms.

Because Pluto is a slow-moving planet remaining up to thirty years in each Sign, it affects an entire generation. It also rules mass movements and great political and social changes. Astrologers talk about Pluto in the Leo generation or the current Pluto in the Capricorn generation.

Chiron

On November 1, 1977 at the Hale Observatory in Pasadena, California, Charles Kowal discovered a new body in our solar system that was later named Chiron. Chiron had a highly eccentric, elliptical orbit mostly between Saturn and Uranus, taking 51 years to make its path around the Sun. To Kowal, Chiron was an unusual body in that it was too large to be a comet and much too bright to be a minor planet. It is an unusually large comet about 50,000 times the size of a normal comet, about the size of an asteroid.

Since that time, other bodies similar to Chiron have also been discovered and classified as the Centaurs. (In mythology, Chiron was a centaur, a half man/half horse creature and was called the wounded healer.)

Because Chiron and the other Centaurs' discoveries are so recent, as far as I am concerned, we astrologers are still in the process of observing how their meaning unfolds. However, by looking at issues and events that occurred during the time of Chiron's discovery, as well as its mythology and observations of how it is affecting clients in their astrology charts, astrologers are gaining more insight into its role as the "wounded healer."

What is meant by the "wounded healer?" It is a pattern where people tend to go back and repeat their self-wounding habits just because this wound still needs healing. I have certainly experienced this in my own life. In the process of going back to the wound, we feel the pain, but after a few times, we eventually learn to stop this habit because it is so painful! Gradually, we learn to stop the bad habit and can come out of it stronger and with a greater understanding.

Barbara Hand Clow, in her book *Chiron: Rainbow Bridge Between the Inner and Outer Planets* considers Chiron a planet and said, *"Chiron is the teacher of the Earth connection to the higher planes and the planetary sighting indicates the time has come to manifest our divinity."*

There is much information about Chiron, but personally, after having analyzed it for years and read research on its influence, I feel I am only just beginning to understand what Chiron is about. However, I do believe that this is indeed the time for us to manifest our divinity; and I also believe that the discovery of new planets is a highly significant event in our history.

Minor Planets, Asteroids, and Comets

At the time of this writing, there have been over 100 minor planets officially discovered in our solar system that are similar to Chiron, Nessus, and Pholus. It has been theorized that Chiron and the Centaurs are objects that escaped from what is known as the Kuiper Belt that contains a disk of objects orbiting beyond Pluto.

Every so often, one of these objects from the Kuiper Belt breaks its orbit and comes into our solar system, like wanderers or messengers bringing their influence for a while and then returning. I believe that all the planets are evolved, living intelligences and that nothing happens by chance.

As for Pholus and Nessus, there is not a great deal of information available about them yet. An increasing number of astrologers are developing an understanding of the meaning of these minor planets. What happens traditionally among astrologers is that, when a new planet is discovered, there is a review of what is happening on Earth at the time of its discovery. However, I say it is too soon, certainly for me, to comment or use them in my work.

Many astrologers are now interpreting minor transiting bodies such as asteroids like Ceres, Juno, Pallas, and Vesta. However, again, they seem highly specific and I have always felt, and still do, that the major planets are the ones who deal with the major issues in our lives. I also happen to believe that the reason astrology works is because the planets are living, breathing, highly evolved Intelligences. Because of this, they radiate their wonderful Energies through this solar system and beyond, helping all life streams to evolve. The asteroids, in my view, are chunks of lifeless rock; so I think astrologers are wasting their time worrying too much about them.

The Ascendant

Obviously, the Ascendant is not a planet but important enough to mention in this Chapter. The spiritual astrologer views the Ascendant, also known as *The Rising Sign*, as the soul's purpose and the force of the soul. Through the sign of the zodiac rising at the time of birth, one can learn the overall goal to be strived for in this life. Alice Bailey describes the Ascendant as *"The Sun of Possibility."* It is here that we see the path we are to take—the Spiritual struggle that awaits us in our transformation from lower self to higher self.

Your Ascendant is the filter through which you interact with your environment; it represents your physical body and indicates health tendencies; it is the first impression you make on others.

It is like a mask or shield that you put on so that you can interact safely with your environment and the people around you. Think of it as a role you play. It is how you are typecast by your family as a child. You may be the popular, glittering Leo Ascendant who aunts adore, or the pretty Libra rising who always says the right thing. Your Ascendant is how you present yourself to the outside world. It is actually like a filter through which the energies of the planets are focused on the material plane. It is like a protective covering you wear, the uniform you take off in private. Without your Ascendant to protect your self-esteem, you feel naked.

Spiritually, it is the point at which we begin to master our environment rather than be controlled by it. It is our potential for this incarnation.

So while the planets are like a cosmic symphony that inter-weave and play different notes to awaken our souls, the Ascendant is a filter for these energies. In this next Chapter, we will complete the planetary picture with the wonderful energies that affect us so deeply from the planet we touch every day of our lives—Mother Earth.

SECTION II

EARTH'S INFLUENCE IN YOUR HOROSCOPE

Chapter 5

Locating the Earth in Your Horoscope

"That which is on its way comes as a cloud which veils the Sun. But hid behind this cloud of immanence is love, and on the Earth is love and in the heaven is love, and this — the love which maketh all things new — must stand revealed."
— Alice Bailey, *Esoteric Psychology*

"My view of our planet was a glimpse of divinity."
— Dr. Edgar Mitchell, Apollo 14 astronaut, *The Way of the Explorer*, 1996.

Astrologers, apart from a few exceptions, have not yet taken into the account the influence of Planet Earth when analyzing horoscopes. There is quite an interest now in reaching deeper into Space and analyzing even the asteroids, while missing the very foundation of our lives, the Mother Earth. Interestingly though, this question about the Earth, although ignored by most astrologers, is one that is frequently asked by students at lectures, classes, and workshops. It is strange that the experts are missing something that the average person can see quite clearly.

It is difficult to locate any information regarding the astrological influence of this planet we call home. It is perhaps not surprising because, until only a few decades ago, when the photographs of the Earth were taken from Space, planet Earth had never been seen or experienced in the heavens by humanity. We view the heavens from our location on Earth Herself. To put it simply, traditional astrology is geocentric (the Earth at the center) because we are *born* on Earth. We're interpreting the Universe from our perspective, our vantage point. We know full well that the Sun is the center of the Solar system (heliocentric);

but we are born on Earth, and we take notice of the influence of the planets from our perspective on planet Earth.

This is primarily because, as mentioned in previous Chapters, we have dissociated ourselves from the Goddess upon whom we live. Despite the fact that the Earth is not traditionally or currently a planet that is observed by astrologers, except a very few, it plays a vitally important role in Spiritual Astrology. This approach puts spirituality front and center, and everything else after that. It is based on the premise that we are spiritual beings first and foremost, learning and, hopefully, evolving on this material plane in physical bodies.

The Earth is of particular importance to those of us who are concerned with the spiritual evolution of our clients—and humanity as a whole—and who use astrology as a tool to help a person to grow spiritually through their lessons, challenges, and opportunities.

Why Have We Missed Planet Earth?

I believe we have missed Planet Earth in our horoscopes because the majority of people are not yet using its positive, astrological influence. In other words, because most people are concerned exclusively with survival and security on this physical plane, rather than yearning to find their spiritual path or expressing their souls through service, they are not yet using this beautiful power of Mother Earth being offered to us.

The time to do so is now. When we look at the state of the world today and see the poverty and massive depletion of natural resources, it is clear that materialism and all its effects, is not the answer. It is more essential today than ever that a critical mass of people are guided by their spiritual selves to give service to others, to help transform the world and to help protect Mother Earth Herself. If we do have this yearning and become conscious of the fact the Mother Earth is an advanced living Intelligence, we shall then, I believe, begin to reconnect with the Earth and so utilize the wonderful energy that She freely offers us. The influence and spiritual power of Mother Earth is readily available to us all. We only have to realize that it is there and then understand and use it.

Very few astrologers have tackled the all-important influence of Mother Earth, but many enjoy the intellectual stimulation of trying to decipher the meaning of asteroids, fixed stars, and so forth. I have to admit that the analyses I offer in the next Chapter, although based on my practice and study of astrology for over forty years, as well as my intuition, is certainly not the *"be all and end all."* My desire is that this book will stimulate an important dialogue so that astrologers and people generally will become more conscious of the Earth and will desire to re-establish a deeper, soul connection with Her—our Divine Mother.

The Earth in Astrology—Ruler of Taurus and Sagittarius

In Spiritual Astrology, the Earth, while being the planet that rules the sign of Taurus on the more basic level, is also the esoteric ruler of the sign of Sagittarius. Several of the planets rule two signs of the zodiac, and the Earth is no exception.

As the esoteric ruler of Sagittarius, the sign of the archer who points towards the path of initiation (Capricorn) with his bow and arrow, the Earth represents a person's Spiritual Path. In Spiritual Astrology, this is, therefore, one of the most important planets—especially at this crucial time of crossroads in our history. It is now becoming increasingly obvious that humanity must leave behind a purely selfish, materialistic life, to embrace a more selfless life of love and service to others for us to sustain our future.

The Position of the Earth in your Horoscope

I say Earth is *one* of the most important planets because as described in the previous Chapter, they are all important. We learn that the Sun represents your creativity, vitality, and the expression of your Soul. Without the energies of the Sun, there would be no life in this Solar System. Interestingly, the Earth is always located exactly opposite the Sun in your natal chart; and because of this, it's simple to find Earth's location, for it is always exactly 180 degrees from the Sun. If for example, you are a Taurus (Sun in Taurus), the Earth in your horoscope will be Scorpio, the opposite sign. If you are Gemini, the Earth will be in Sagittarius. If you happen to know the exact position of the Sun in your horoscope i.e., Aries at 27 degrees 52 minutes, then the Earth will be exactly opposite at Libra 27 degrees 52 minutes.

Although there is at least one other theory about where the Earth is located in your horoscope, this to me is the most logical and esoterically significant position. Without the life-giving energies of the Sun, we could not exist here on Earth, let alone tread the Spiritual Path represented by the Earth. It is when we center ourselves in our Sun energies and then walk the Spiritual Path represented by the Earth, that we can make great Spiritual progress.

There is also a strong connection between the planet Saturn and the Earth. Saturn represents the karma we are here to experience. Our karma is a result of all our actions and thoughts of the past and manifests as opportunities presented and challenges to be met. The Earth represents our dharma, for instance, the way we go about doing this. If for example, we had become too self-centered over several lifetimes, and we are born with Saturn in Aries highlighting these lessons and the Earth in Virgo, these planetary influences may lead us to the Path of Service where we learn to give, expecting nothing in return.

Planetary Rulers

In astrology, each Sign of the Zodiac has a ruling planet. These rulers influence the different signs and were assigned to the twelve different signs from Aries to Pisces before Uranus,

Neptune, and Pluto were discovered. These classical rulers are still used by some astrologers, including myself. For example, the Moon rules Cancer, and the Sun rules Leo, and so on.

Note also that several of the planets rule two Signs of the Zodiac (i.e., Mercury is the planetary ruler of Gemini and Virgo); Mars rules both Aries and is the co-ruler of Scorpio; Venus rules Taurus and Libra; Jupiter rules Sagittarius and is the co-ruler of Pisces; Saturn rules Capricorn and is the co-ruler of Aquarius. I believe that Chiron is the co-ruler of Virgo, though that is not accepted by all astrologers.

Now we also have Earth as the ruler of both Taurus and Sagittarius. The planets that are now the exoteric rulers of the twelve Signs of the Zodiac are, therefore, as follows:

Sign of the Zodiac	Ruling Planet(s)
Aries	Mars
Taurus	Venus and Earth
Gemini	Mercury
Cancer	Moon
Leo	Sun
Virgo	Mercury and Chiron
Libra	Venus
Scorpio	Pluto and Mars
Sagittarius	Jupiter and Earth
Capricorn	Saturn
Aquarius	Uranus and Saturn
Pisces	Jupiter and Neptune

Why Astrology Works

There are many rationales for why Astrology works. My own belief, through years of study of astrology and metaphysics is that the planets are living Intelligences, far more evolved than we are. As evolved Intelligences, they are constantly radiating their light, love, and power throughout this solar system, creating a divine interplay of cosmic energies — an harmonious symphony of energy designed to help all life to evolve.

Since we have freewill to think, feel, and act as we choose, on the whole we do not use these wonderful, liberating energies in the way we could. The result is that we may feel that the planetary transits are difficult, uncomfortable, and harsh. It is only when we resist this divine symphony leading us to true freedom that we feel the pressure as uncomfortable, difficult and painful; but actually the pressure is urging us towards our Higher Selves, if only we realize it.

Chapter 6

Earth Signs – Earth's Influence through the Signs of the Zodiac

"When the night is dark, may you have faith that the Sun will rise in so short a time.

May compassion inspire you to action, and the enduring Love of God fuel your inner fire.

May your relationships—human, animal, the Blessed Mother Earth, the Great Ones who watch over us—be filled with grace and love."

—C. Blaze

This Chapter is about the influence of the planet Earth and the power and potential it offers us, if we are prepared to consciously use this power and strength. We have been told by astrologers how to inhabit and draw upon the creativity of our Sun Signs and this is vitally important. Now, it takes an even more self-aware person to also utilize the power of what I call our "Earth Sign."

However, before we look at the Earth Signs, i.e., influence of the Earth in each of the twelve signs of the zodiac, let us first look at the underlying influence of the Earth and what this means to us.

Earth's Influence

The Earth—being exactly opposite to the Sun which represents our creativity, character and our vitality—offers us a concrete way to develop creativity and character and to use our vitality on the physical plane of this beautiful planet.

As the planetary ruler of Taurus, the builder, the Earth helps us to build our dreams through action on this world in which we live. The more we attune to the element of Earth, the more we feel an urge to make positive things happen rather than just thinking about them, wishing for them or dreaming about them. It is the energy that helps us to bring our aspirations to life and to translate our compassion and love for others into practical acts of service for humanity.

Like all the planets, the more we advance and evolve as individuals, the higher aspects of the planets we attract to ourselves. Earth is also the esoteric ruler of Sagittarius, the sign of the visionary; the person focused on their goals to create their future. The energy of Earth can facilitate this: at a higher level it is our Spiritual Path.

In other words, while the Sun represents our character—who we are becoming and our self-realization—the Earth is the path that allows us expression of ourselves through practical deeds.

Like all the planets, the Earth is here helping us to evolve but because we actually live on the Earth, it offers us the way to express our heart's desires. We should not take this for granted for, unlike the other planets, we are blessed to be able to directly attune to Earth's energies through being in the nurturing presence of Her fruits—Nature. Whether we are by a lake, river or an ocean, or amidst the trees and mountains, we can actually attune ourselves to the living Intelligence beneath our very feet. The more we become conscious of Earth's energies, the more we can find our Path, as well as the power and strength to live up to this.

There is also a strong connection between the planet Saturn and the Earth. Saturn represents the karma we are here to experience. Our karma is a result of all our actions and thoughts of the past and manifests as opportunities presented and challenges to be met. The Earth represents our dharma, i.e., the way we go about doing this.

Earth, as a planet, is a mighty Cosmic Intelligence who nurtures us and gives us all we need in our journey through evolution. She is a verdant planet, beautiful and green with vast blue oceans and it is not by chance that she is referred to as Mother Earth. She offers to us the nurturing, loving, compassionate energy of the best Mother you could have. She gives to us everything in Her power to sustain, feed, nurture and heal us – with no thought of reward. When we attune to Earth's power at a deep level we feel this great Love that She offers to us and once we accept this Love energy into our own hearts and souls, there is no end to the miracles we can achieve on this beautiful planet – miracles that can heal others, as well as heal and transform our world. Earth's energies are urging us to embrace a more selfless life of love and service to others in order to sustain our future.

You could, therefore, look at your Earth Sign as representing the field or type of service (the grounding of the soul on this material plane) that your soul will guide you towards in this life, if you allow it. You may be drawn to healing; you may have a desire to help those less fortunate; or you may wish to be involved in animal rescue or environmental causes. There are many ways to serve on this planet, and the Sun's energies provide us with the energy and vitality to do this. The Earth shows us our Spiritual Path and what form this can take. This is not to limit us, but to help us express our divine potential more fully.

Sun Signs and Earth Signs

When we center ourselves in our Sun Sign and then walk the Spiritual Path represented by our opposite Earth Sign, we can find true balance in our lives. Once you find your Sun Sign from the table below, you will find your Earth Sign opposite.

Earth Sign	Sun Sign
Aries	Libra
Taurus	Scorpio
Gemini	Sagittarius
Cancer	Capricorn
Leo	Aquarius

Virgo	Pisces
Libra	Aries
Scorpio	Taurus
Sagittarius	Gemini
Capricorn	Cancer
Aquarius	Leo
Pisces	Virgo

The Secret of Using Your Earth Sign Power

The secret of using the power of your Earth Sign is to become aware of their different energies within you and attempt to use them and manifest them as positively as possible. Since the Sun and Earth are opposite each other in your birth chart, you may always feel this pull, as if your life is somewhat of a balancing act. Well, life is indeed a balancing act, but it is always good to remember that the Sun is the center of this solar system, and it is also the center of our lives.

First, try and center yourself in the positive attributes of your Sun Sign (you may find more in my book *Superstar Signs*, or another good astrology book on the Sun Signs) and from there, draw and use the power of your Earth Sign and the power of the other planets.

For example, if you have the Sun in sensitive, cautious Cancer, express this side of yourself through a group, family, or friends; but also don't neglect to use the great power of your Earth in the opposite Capricorn. For an enlightened Cancer, they will not be satisfied with a purely personal life, but will be ambitious to achieve, strive, and reach their spiritual goals. In other words, the more aware person will naturally use the power of their Earth Sign; for others, it is a learning process.

The following analyses of the different Earth Sign/Sun Sign combinations is designed to help you to become more aware of this great potential and power that is ours to take in our journey through evolution. Not only does the Mother Earth feed, heal, and nurture us, but She also enables us to evolve spiritually upon Her beautiful body.

Earth in Aries/Sun in Libra

A person born with the Earth in Aries has the Sun in the opposite sign of Libra. As these are two Cardinal signs, this combination is all about action and activity. Both Aries and Libra are masculine, Cardinal signs. Aries is Cardinal Fire and Libra is Cardinal Air; but Aries is ruled by the action-packed planet Mars, while Libra is ruled by the peace-loving Venus. To utilize the power and potential of their Earth Sign Aries, this person lives somewhat of a balancing act—striving for peace and harmony with others, while at the same time feeling an inner desire to blaze new trails and enjoying the thrill of the unknown.

When a person is drawing upon and using the potential of his Aries Earth, he will courageously fly high and go where no one has been before. This person, not content just with the discussions and social contacts enjoyed by his Sun in Libra, also likes to work hard and achieve. He enjoys the thrill of the unknown; and, when he reaches his destination, another trail lies before him waiting to blaze. Always seeking distant pastures new, never content, never resting on laurels, and knowing the only place for him is out in front.

Out in front is a lonely place and this can be especially true for the Earth Sign Aries. With their Sun in Libra, they like to spend time around and with people, enjoying social engagements, and seeking peace and harmony rather than trail blazing. While this is important for Earth in Aries, if they become too embroiled in the thoughts and ideas of others, they can lose their keen focus and intelligent perspective.

This combination is all about achieving balance. This person is learning who they are at a deep level; they are learning when to assert themselves; and when to resolve conflict and work in a team. If this balance isn't achieved, there will always be a certain tension that may eventually manifest in the physical body. These are individuals who need to learn to relax, to socialize, to listen and share with others, while never losing their own unique focus.

It is especially essential to maintain health of body, mind and spirit, and it is helpful for Earth in Aries people to spend time in Nature. At these times, they need to take the journey alone or with people who are closely attuned to their ideals. They are especially drawn to the mountains and sacred places and can draw spiritual strength from these places. These places stimulate their highest aspirations and here inspirations are born. They find great solace in the rocks and mountains. It is important for them to get away from the hustle and bustle of everyday life from time to time.

Earth in Aries people who are awakened to the power of the living Mother Earth can have a genius for understanding Her and the beauties of Nature. They can find their own center in the power of the Earth; and it is here that they can analyze their ideas alone, away from the input of others. If their ideas are strong and true with a core of spirituality, and an element of practicality to make them work, they can be successful and powerful enough to make a positive difference to themselves, and to the world around them.

Earth in Aries has a strong mind and a strong will, so he should be careful that his ideas do not run away with him. If these are not grounded with a positive and selfless motive, he can bring confusion and even devastation to himself and others. It is especially important for Earth in Aries to learn to control his mind and his thoughts, and a discipline such as meditation is very helpful to him.

The inclination with impulsive Aries is to want things to happen instantly, quickly, immediately. With Earth in Aries, this tendency can be tamed by retreats into Nature or by understanding how an idea is like a seed that must be watered, fed, and slowly nurtured by the light of the Sun and the slow movement of the seasons for it to blossom in the right way. Grounding is essential for Earth in Aries for progress to be made.

When fully grounded, Earth in Aries can make a fine leader, often active in environmental causes, or ecology in all its forms. The awakened Earth in Aries cannot justify the mindless taking of resources from the Earth, and he is a person who is prepared to fight to stop things like fracking, water privatization, or to spread the message of spiritual ecology—whatever it takes to try and restore the balance and harmony that is the essence of their opposite planet—the Sun in Libra.

With Earth in Aries people, there is a natural inclination towards the Hermetic axiom *"Man, know thyself!"* The enlightened Earth in Aries realizes that when he discovers who he really is at a deep level, then he can give himself to a cause bigger and nobler than he is. He knows that when he surrenders himself to something more important than him alone that this will truly bring freedom.

The self-centered quality associated with the often misunderstood Sign of Aries can be transformed with the Earth in Aries into something of great value to not only themselves but to the world. Some may think this innate desire to know and understand themselves and their limits is ego; actually, in the evolved Aries, it is not ego at all. It is the urge for self-understanding so that self-control and mastery can be achieved. With Aries, the so-called *selfishness* can become transmuted into selflessness more than with any other sign.

Because of this innate drive towards self-understanding, combined with a desire to develop their talents, skills, and resources, they are often driven to push their limits through physical activity, as well as mental challenges and spiritual practices. They find stability in being physically active and can become great athletes with stamina and desire to set goals and accomplish these. Their heroes are often people of great strength—whether physical, mental, or spiritual. They particularly admire a figure like Mahatma Gandhi, who sought peace and justice through acts of great courage and strength. Deep down, these people want the peace and harmony of the opposite sign of their Sun in Libra, but they instinctively know that to achieve peace requires standing up for what is right and being prepared to fight for it.

They want to know how far they can go and so they like to push the limits. The enlightened Earth in Aries with the fire of spiritual desire burning with them can go a long way in this lifetime towards manifesting their divine potential.

When they truly find out who they are, people with the Earth in Aries are among the most sincere people you could meet. Their opposite influence of Sun in Libra can at times be caught up in politics and power plays with others. However, with this combination of Sun in Libra and Earth in Aries, regular retreats will literally bring them down to Earth—to the place where they are sure of their own hearts, minds, and souls. It is when they are centered in this place that they can be true to themselves and their own guiding principles. These regular retreats do not necessarily have to be out in Nature or the mountainous regions they love so much; they can be spiritual retreats in their own homes. Regular retreats, wherever they take place, are essential for Earth in Aries.

Earth in Aries knows how the world works and how games and power plays are a part of it; they can play these games with the best of them. Deep down, however, they are not into playing games, behaving perfectly, or fitting in.

However, self-knowledge alone is not enough. Enlightened Earth in Aries people are aware of their deep connections to others—to humanity as a whole, to the Earth who sustains them, and to the God within. One of their spiritual tasks is to bring an idea to Earth; an idea that will be of practical, spiritual value to others. They are inspired to share what they have found with others—whether these are ideas, or literally pieces of sacred rocks or stones they may find on their journeys. It is in these places of Nature that Earth in Aries gains strength; learns independence and the realization that, at the end of the day, they can rely on nobody but themselves.

The combination of Earth in Aries and Sun in Libra results in a person of high ideals. It is our ideals that move us to fight for our downtrodden fellow man, or to be inspired by a noble vision. When Aries in Earth joins his ideals with his intuition, bathed in the fires of courageous actions, then he will be the spiritual warrior he is meant to be, courageously working for peace on this planet despite the personal cost to himself.

Here is a person who realizes that peace on Earth is the goal, but Earth in Aries knows that peace will not come without action. He is here to shine light into the darkness and dispel the bats of ignorance through expressing his fine intellect and espousing noble causes. He knows that peace will not come while greed and selfishness prevail. He is here to fight every act of pettiness, jealousy, and anger that burns within his own heart—bringing the victory of his higher nature over his lower. This too is his quest.

Above all, Earth in Aries is action personified. Right action to restore our relationship with Mother Earth is one of the highest and most noble paths for him in these days. Although it is essential for Earth in Aries to follow his own inner voice, he realizes that greater victories can be won by working with others of like mind while at the same time never allowing others to dampen his high intelligence and noble spirit.

This combination of Mars-ruled Aries and Venus-ruled Libra is here learning discipline and also love. He is inclined to be hard on himself but is learning that, while discipline is essential, he also must love, cherish and value himself as well as others.

The key for Earth in Aries is to put his high ideals and noble ideas into action—then the world will be his oyster. For the evolved Earth in Aries, his impulses—born from his higher nature—will lead him unerringly to where he is meant to be.

The Earth as Co-Ruler of Taurus

The Earth and the sign of Taurus have a strong connection because the Earth is, I believe, the ruling planet of this Sign together with Venus. The Earth is also the co-ruler of the Sign of Sagittarius. Although I bow to the far greater wisdom of The Master Djwal Khul and his teaching in *Esoteric Astrology*, I do not know enough about the planet Vulcan to assign this planet as the co-ruler of the sign of Taurus, as this Ascended Master does. Right now for me, everything points towards The Earth. I will remain with this, but also will remain open to the possibility that I am only seeing a part of the picture.

The science and art of Astrology, like Astronomy, is constantly evolving as more and more planets and asteroids are discovered almost weekly. I think we astrologers do the best we can to keep up with the changes; but I feel, at this moment in time, the co-ruler of Taurus is Mother Earth.

There needs to be much more emphasis on the Earth. This analysis of the Earth in Taurus may play a part in reorienting people born under this Sign, and this will help to re-establish the close connection they have with the Earth upon which we live. This is a particularly important time, therefore, for those born with a strong Taurus or Sagittarian influence in their horoscopes. Of course, with great opportunity comes great responsibility.

Previously, Venus has been considered the sole ruler of the sign of Taurus. This makes sense because the sign of Taurus, although a practical sign of the earth element (different from Planet Earth) and fixed in nature, very often has the artistic flair of a Venus-ruled person. Earth as a co-ruler is ideal because the two planets Earth and Venus have a very special connection from an esoteric perspective.

In *The Secret Doctrine*, the magnum opus of the great

theosophist and occultist, Madame Blavatsky, states:

Every sin committed on Earth is felt in Venus. Every change in Venus is reflected on Earth.

There is a psychic link between the planetary Logos of Venus and that of our Earth.
The Venus scheme is more active than ours.
Its humanity are more advanced than ours.

Earth in Taurus/Sun in Scorpio

A person born with the Earth in Taurus has the Sun in the opposite sign of Scorpio. These are both feminine Fixed signs, and this combination is all about loyalty and perseverance. Taurus is fixed earth and Scorpio is fixed water. Taurus is ruled by Venus and also by the Earth (see previous section: 'The Earth: Co-Ruler of Taurus'). Scorpio is ruled by both Mars and Pluto.

People born with the Earth in Taurus are of the element of earth, grounded on this physical plane. This is good because it is on this plane of existence that we can learn the most and evolve the most. These are people who are aware of their resources and know how to use them; they can accomplish a lot; they are organized, determined, reliable, and responsible. They enjoy the security of routine and do not want to be pushed or rushed.

The opposite Sign of Scorpio urges people to experience the emotional and spiritual depths of life. However, the opposite Earth in Taurus can provide a good balance for passionate Scorpio. Taurus is very much at home in the physical world, the world of the senses and of Nature. This provides a good balance for Scorpio, and they can draw upon the common sense and practicality of their Earth in Taurus to help steer them away from emotional excess.

If an enlightened Scorpio is on a powerful spiritual path, he can use his Earth in Taurus to ground him through regular spiritual practices or regular charitable acts. This regularity that Taurus understands so well, helps Scorpio to manifest his ideals and follow his dreams and spiritual goals without veering off the path that has been set.

When drawing on the vitality of Sun in Scorpio and following the promptings of their soul, as expressed by Earth in Taurus, these people find their strength and their depth through expressing themselves in practical ways. They can transform the passion and deep feelings of Scorpio into practical acts of service for others.

Earth in Taurus is connected to the natural world and the rhythms of the cycles and seasons. There is a need for this person to be in contact with nature or natural things, and may find himself or herself gardening, hiking, or using their innate artistic ability to paint, draw, or write. Sun in Scorpio people may not consider themselves artistic, but when they draw upon the power of their Earth in Taurus, they can find a great deal of artistic potential. They can also express this in other ways, such as through creative thinking or singing or dancing. They also have an artistic flair for working with their hands, such as carpentry or playing a musical instrument.

Earth in Taurus has a strong affinity with Mother Earth and her fruits—Nature. When this person is stressed and overwhelmed, he can find a certain peace in nature that will help to ground his passionate nature and improve his health. Earth in Taurus people should regularly feel the Earth under their feet. It is therapeutic for them to hike or walk in nature and to be aware of the trees, the plants, as well as the spirits of nature that take care of the blossoming of a rose or the sprouting of seeds.

People with Sun in Scorpio and Earth in Taurus have a great deal of feeling for nature and the nature spirits or devas. While they may not see the devas or smell their perfume as some people do, when they spend time in alone in nature, they will be aware of them and feel their presence. If their Earth in Taurus is not expressed, they may feel a craving for material things—such as money or food—but this can also be satisfied by a stronger connection with the Earth.

These individuals may be surprised at how easily they can establish a rapport with the unseen forces by offering their gratitude and thanks for the tireless work of these fantastic but very real elementals, nature spirits, and the great devas of the mountains, the oceans, and the forests. This will bring to them a certain satisfaction, a feeling of soul fulfillment, and some peace to the turbulence that is often so much a part of this passionate person's life.

When Sun in Scorpio draws upon the power of the Earth in Taurus, they find tremendous strength: their strength is enduring like that of an oak tree. This part of their nature, when expressed, is beautiful like the cherry blossom in May, the Taurus month of the year. This strong connection with the beauty and abundance of nature leads them at some point on their spiritual journey to want to connect with Mother Earth at a deep soul level. They may yearn to go into the mountains or deep into a cave. This seems to still their passionate emotional nature and bring the peace and stillness that they crave. If they are unable to do this on a regular basis, it is important for them to find this inner peace through contemplating upon the Earth and offering their gratitude to Her.

This connection with nature may not come naturally, as they are often caught up in the emotional crises that Sun in Scorpio seems to attract. However, evolution comes through becoming more conscious and aware. Since the Earth is the ruler of the sign of Taurus, this 'Earth consciousness' is essential for Earth in Taurus more than any other sign. When their emotions are out of balance, they can find peace and solace through the beauty and strength of Mother Earth. They may hug a tree to feel and attune to the life sap coursing through it, or plant their feet firmly on the earth and feel the breeze ruffling their hair.

When life becomes tough for Earth in Taurus, it is very healing for them to visualize the great Violet Flame that comes from the Logos of the Planet whenever requested—strengthening, purifying, uplifting, and spiritualizing.[5]

Earth in Taurus people often face many trials and challenges while learning the self-mastery and control that is so essential for them. These difficult challenges of life that they seem to face more than most can pull them away from their high ideals or their spiritual path towards a purely materialistic approach. In the long run though, this will not satisfy them and will bring them frustration. While they have a talent for making and manipulating money and have practical skills that are essential in this material world, it is also essential for their soul growth to ground their powerful emotional natures regularly. Earth in Taurus can do this by working to preserve the planet through growing their own food or recycling; and, more importantly, by giving thanks and appreciation to the Mother Earth in one of many ways.

Another way for them to find balance is to transmute the emotional energy and vitality of their Sun in Scorpio through some type of spiritual discipline—whether that is working in charitable ways or regular Spiritual practices. The person with Earth in Taurus is reliable enough to set up a schedule and stick to it no matter what.

This combination of Taurus and Scorpio also has strength, as well as physical magnetism. We are all healers, but Earth in Taurus people can be particularly magnetic and powerful healers. Once they learn a technique that makes sense to them, they are able to channel their deep feelings into love and empathy for others in a disciplined way and direct the universal life forces through themselves more easily than most. Healing and prayer are other ways for them to bring balance to their lives. They can transmute the intense passions that sometimes lead them in the wrong direction into a certain inner peace for themselves, as well as compassion for others.

Earth in Taurus people may appear silent and controlled most of the time, but they do have a temper; and although they may not lose it very often, it's just so memorable that it's important to note!

While these people can be extremely pleasant, charming, and reliable, it is important never to think of them as weak. This is why Earth in Taurus needs to channel their energies in ways that suggest strength and longevity. They are builders, good at maintaining and sustaining what others have already started. Rather than initiating new projects, they can accomplish this in a reliable, responsible way. They are here on Earth to build and leave behind them a lasting monument—one born from their deep emotions and spiritual yearning of their Scorpio Sun.

For example, as physically magnetic healers, they could build a healing sanctuary in a significant sacred area of Earth, where others could come and receive healing into the future. The awakened Earth in Taurus could help to build an organization dedicated to preserving the Earth or support an advanced ecological Mission, such as Operation Sunbeam. [6]

Although we live in a complex technological age, Earth in Taurus doesn't enjoy complications. He is attuned to simplicity and enjoys the inevitability of the seasons and the endless rhythms of Nature. It is here that he will find peace. As well as having a complex feeling nature, there is also a certain simplicity about him. He has a way of speaking that gets straight to the point with common sense and bluntness. His practical intelligence helps him to thrive and succeed in careers that involve persistence, stability, and relentless drive.

Earth in Taurus has the ability to express and communicate feelings in a way that few can. Through their Sun in Scorpio, they can intuit how others are feeling; and then, drawing on the power of their Earth in Taurus, they can express and communicate these feelings, sincerely and simply. They can do this verbally, through writing poetry and verse, song, or the spoken word; or creatively through artwork, photography, cooking, or crafts.

This particular combination often seems to attract to themselves difficult, complex, and complicated relationships that take up a lot of their time and energy. In some ways, they would rather have this than no relationship at all, because security is very important to this person. They are here learning the value of commitment in all areas of life, and at times may have to endure endless routine work to find the end result of greater security. This is a learning lesson for Earth in Taurus, and they often learn through pain and suffering. They learn that anything worthwhile takes time, effort, patience, energy, and it does not happen overnight.

An Earth in Taurus person has a highly attuned value system, and he is here on Earth learning how to live these values, not just as idealistic concepts. But also, he is using them in practical, useful, common-sense ways that add richness, beauty, comfort, and spirituality to life. He is learning to move away from reacting emotionally to things that disturb and upset him, towards embodying and living old-fashioned but enduring values. The enlightened Earth in Taurus realizes that integrity and ethical behavior is, at the end of the day, far more fulfilling than superficial pleasures.

He is learning to value honor above political acumen, candor and honesty above a clever tongue, and common sense and wisdom above intellect. He has a generous heart, and although he may not be moved to tears by the plight of the world, he is prepared to roll up his sleeves and work hard to help those less fortunate. His vision of beauty, comfort, and safety is not just for him, but for everyone in the world; and he will play his part to make this happen.

Earth in Taurus needs to be rooted firmly on this physical plane because it is here he can accomplish his dreams and bring them into manifestation.

Earth in Gemini/Sun in Sagittarius

A person born with the Earth in Gemini has the Sun in the opposite sign of Sagittarius. As these are two mutable signs, this combination is all about change and flexibility. Both Gemini and Sagittarius are masculine mutable signs. Gemini is mutable Air, and Sagittarius is mutable Water. The Earth in Gemini person is learning how to ground the innate wisdom and intuition of his opposite sign of Sagittarius through right knowledge and communication. He is learning about all the different paths, and it's important to him to be open to others' points of view and to ground his intellect and intuition through study of the higher truths.

Earth in Gemini people are born with a mission or quest for the meaning of life, but sometimes it takes them a while to find out exactly what it is and how to express it. This desire to know is with them from childhood, and one of the first questions of this curious child is often "Why?" The awakened Earth in Gemini will spend the rest of their lives finding answers to the deeper questions of life, i.e., "Why are we here on Earth and what is our true purpose?"

Earth in Gemini people can ground their natural adventurous spirit and desire to know the truth through sharing their knowledge with others. They enjoy collecting information, gathering facts, and then disseminating what they have learned. Because of this, they make excellent teachers (if they can overcome the desire to preach to others that their way is the only way). Also, they can become easily bored if things seem too difficult or if they are presented with too many choices. Once they find the Truth, however, they can be so enthusiastic and inspired that they feel then they can overcome any difficulties in its pursuit.

With the enlightened Earth in Gemini, truth to them is everything and they may spend their entire lifetime seeking it. This person is here learning open-mindedness, diversity, understanding, and tolerance. This helps them to realize that they cannot force other people to accept what they know to be true! They realize that everyone has their path to follow, and we are all learning. They have high ideals, and they like everything to be above board and straightforward. However, life is not like that; and sometimes a more subtle, intelligently thought-out approach achieves the best results.

By understanding the diversity of life by talking to and studying people from different cultures and backgrounds, Earth in Gemini finds the solace that is so needed by this busy, energetic, larger-than-life combination. Once they truly understand diversity, they will no longer expect or desire others to be like them. This can be gained by a deep study of the Law of Karma, and suddenly everything that appeared to be so out-of-balance and unfair, becomes just. Nothing is what it seems, and this is a lesson for Earth in Gemini. This understanding will give them peace of mind.

They have a strong affinity with Mother Earth and, with their innate global outlook, they have love and respect for all life: nations, animals, and nature in all its forms. It is essential that they not only express this global outlook without prejudice, but also find a way to ground their love of all through service to humanity. Through offering themselves in service, they do not have to like everyone, approve of anyone, or wish everyone was like themselves—but in this way, they can express love and feel compassion for all. This will in turn broaden their outlook and bring them the joy and enthusiasm that is the fuel for this combination of Earth in Gemini/Sun in Sagittarius.

With their large global outlook, there is a need to learn as much as they can about different countries and lifestyles to expand their own worldview. These people are often humanitarians who care as much about people in another country as in their own backyard. An injustice to a person across the other side of the world is just as painful to these large-hearted individuals as injustices to themselves. You will often see the enlightened Earth in Gemini supporting and promoting global causes.

Life never stands still for Earth in Gemini. They need always to be on the move—not by wasting time in endless, meaningless pursuits that can lead them away from their main purpose, but by constantly learning about themselves, the purpose of life, and the world around them. They can do this by becoming more receptive and open to new knowledge and by being prepared to tackle the details rather than just enjoying the big picture which their opposite Sun in Sagittarius can see so clearly.

A person with the Sun in Sagittarius/Earth in Gemini is an adventurer at heart. Quite often he will travel the world and live in a different country from that in which he was born. His global outlook is developed through this spirit. If this person stops moving and learning and finds his present circumstances restricting, he can balance himself through spending time in nature, and through Spiritual disciplines such as meditation. By finding stillness, he will learn that all knowledge, all wisdom, and all freedom lay within. When he realizes that, he will also realize that he no longer needs to travel the world to find what he has been seeking.

Earth in Gemini is often fun to be around; they are full of life and energy and have a positive approach. They have a visionary quality, but they should avoid excessive idealism and faith based on what they'd like rather than what is. It's important for them to ground their beliefs through their everyday actions. Instead of thinking other people should change the world in this way or that, the lesson is for *them* to be the change. *Change* is the keyword for these individuals, and they have the honesty and flexibility to make changes when they know they need to. Unlike others signs that may get stuck in a rut there is little danger of that with an awakened Earth in Gemini.

An example of how they can live their beliefs may be someone who learns enough about the environment or ecology that they can then share this with others through teaching or leading a movement or group. It is important for this person to draw on their intellectual Earth in Gemini energy to analyze the concrete facts of the situation in an objective way and then present their findings in an intelligent, open-minded fashion to others. Unless they learn to do this, they will not achieve the results they desire. Sun in Sagittarius can be careless and overly zealous but by using the energy of their opposite Earth in Gemini, they are more thoughtful, clever, and able to take into account other people's viewpoints.

They are here to eschew dogma and embrace new revelations. They are here to be open to the wonder and vastness of the Universe and all its myriad expressions. It is when they truly live their vision, with confidence in themselves and the power of their intellect and intuition; that others will respond to them and be inspired by their enthusiasm.

One key for Earth in Gemini people is to put their faith to work. They may feel optimistic about the future on this planet, but unless they roll up their sleeves and work to make a difference, their dreams will not manifest as they envision. Visions without works are meaningless and this is a big lesson for this combination. It is not uncommon for this person to try and then fail, and then try and fail again, and then keep on trying. This is a great quality—a quality of the intrepid adventurer that he is at heart—and helps him to learn and prepare for the next big adventure!

Unlike more cautious souls, they are able to throw themselves into the next opportunity that comes their way with as much enthusiasm as they did the first time. They are ready for miracles and, often to the surprise of their friends and families, miracles often come their way. However, unless they analyze their mistakes, dot the "i's" and cross the "t's" to find out what did not work the first time, they will keep going round and round the same track. They will have their failures and their miracles, but unless they try to understand these, they may experience the same patterns taking place in their lives over and over again. Through honesty and understanding, they can avoid wasting their precious time and energy.

Another wonderful thing about Earth in Gemini is that he has many different sides to his diverse personality, and he is fully alive at all times. While some signs, like Cancer and Scorpio, understand the value of self-protection and are able to go into semi-hibernation during difficult times, Earth in Gemini is "full on" most of the time! This can be hard on him as well as other more sensitive souls in their vicinity.

The best thing for Earth in Gemini is to have plenty of safe, energetic avenues to let off steam. They can be quite sporty, but they like to be free to do what they want to do when they want, rather than to be in a strict physical regime. It's important for them to have some physical activity whether it is biking or hiking, something that they feel good about and enjoy. Although strong and athletic, they can also be clumsy if they don't pay attention to their immediate environment! They like to feel good about themselves and their bodies so that health doesn't impede them or get in the way of their next challenge.

Earth in Gemini is always on the move and doesn't like to stand still for long. They can excel at any type of movement such as intricate dance steps, yoga, or martial arts.

Although honest with an inbuilt code of morals and are trust-worthy and ethical, this combination doesn't like to feel stuck in a job or relationship. They will be happy—and their friends and partners by default—when they are learning, moving, and growing.

Others around them may be worried sick about money, family, mortgages, and healthcare, while often Earth in Gemini will appear with the magic key—a healthy dose of wisdom, positivity, intuition, and faith that is able to put things into perspective. When all hope appears to be gone, they will prove otherwise and inspire you into action and prove to you that miracles are the norm.

At heart, this person has an incredible *joie de vivre,* enthusiasm, confidence, and sense of fun; but he can also be challenging to the more cautious or down-to-earth type. He may at times seem childish in his grand schemes for the future. He can be infuriating when he thinks he knows best and irritating with his blunt manner and homespun philosophy. However, despite all this, it's worth making friends with Sun in Sagittarius/Earth in Gemini because he will take you on a ride to the stars and back—and that will be before breakfast!

More important for Earth in Gemini, even than the physical and mental challenges that will help them channel their vital energy, are the spiritual challenges. It is when they turn their intelligence, wisdom, and intuition inwards to gain greater self-awareness and honest self-knowledge that they really make progress. The enlightened Earth in Gemini understands there is a "Grand Plan" to life; and part of their destiny is to work out not only how to hook themselves up to this, but how to make it work for the benefit of all humanity.

The Earth in Cancer/Sun in Capricorn

A person born with the Earth in Cancer has the Sun in the opposite sign of Capricorn. These are both feminine Cardinal signs, and this combination is all about activity and action. Cancer is Cardinal Water, and Capricorn is Cardinal Earth.

The Earth is exalted in the sign of Cancer; here is a person who will do his best to preserve and protect what is of value to him. This may be his home, his family and, for the enlightened person, the spiritual truths, including Mother Earth and Her resources.

These people may be late bloomers, but once they get going, they can work harder, smarter, and faster than most to achieve their high goals and objectives. Earth in Cancer has many sterling qualities. They are practical, prudent, reliable, ambitious, patient, disciplined, rational, reserved, stable, hardworking, careful, wise, self-conscious, thoughtful, calm, and humorous.

They are certainly worth studying, as their hidden depths reveal an interesting character. They are often very impressed with other people's achievements and will strive to emulate and even surpass them.

As a Sun in Capricorn, this person enjoys people of quality and success, and he likes to spend time with them. After all, if his goal is to be a multi-millionaire, why would he spend time around people with no money? If he strives to be a top Olympic athlete, you won't find him endlessly kicking a football in the local park, but instead he will be studying at the feet of other successful athletes.

When this person awakens to his opposite Earth in Cancer, he finds that balance comes when he begins to develop more fully his feeling nature. He realizes life is not just about scaling the heights of his many goals, but it is also about being prepared to make mistakes, to learn and develop L-O-V-E in the highest sense of the word (as indeed we all are doing , but it is particularly important for this combination).

It is only when Earth in Cancer learns that true value lies within rather than in the outside world, that he will use his real power and incredible potential. Once that realization dawns, he can become a wise, spiritual being, and you may find him studying at the feet of enlightened teachers or Masters.

They prefer that life goes smoothly and nothing interrupts them in their many plans or goals. They like to surround themselves with what makes them feel calm and peaceful. However, all too often they find themselves at the center of an argument or disagreement, trying to sort things out and their peace is disturbed. They care about people and, despite their lofty goals, the awakened Earth in Cancer will always stop on the way up their personal mountaintop to lend a helping hand to someone who has fallen by the wayside.

As soon as they realize that this is how it's meant to be, they will be using even more of their potential. They are learning and growing as compassionate humans, realizing that we are all family. Earth in Cancer may have a large family of their own, but there is always room for more. You might go to their home for a cup of tea and end up being invited to lunch or dinner. Everyone is family to this nurturing sign.

They have a cool, intelligent, calm, and controlled manner. They have great strength and are able to climb the precipices of life, despite the stony ground. They work quietly, steadily, and surely towards their objectives—despite any obstacles. Although they appear to have a strong unconquerable spirit, they also have a deep need for reassurance and appreciation that doesn't always show to those who don't really know or understand them. They may appear to have all the answers, but they also like to seek guidance from experienced and wise people.

Earth in Cancer will naturally care for all who need help. Their kindness draws people to them for solace as well as for wise advice and generous counsel. One of the lessons for this person is to learn how to be vulnerable and allow other people to become close—also to realize that this type of vulnerability is not weakness. In other words, Earth in Cancer is learning to understand the ways of the heart. They may want to give and give to others, but there has to be a balance. Earth in Cancer is also here learning to receive nurturing from others.

Concrete expressions of appreciation appeal to the person with Sun in Capricorn and Earth in Cancer. Don't just tell her how much you appreciate her, but put it in writing. Or, even better, give her a gift however small it may be. If it's a gift from the heart, this person of great control and ability, will probably shed tears of appreciation. Earth in Cancer is shy and hard on herself; and when others praise her efforts, it is music to her ears. However, accolades or not, this person is action-packed and hardworking and will keep going long after other lesser mortals have given up. People may often wonder why this person seems to win the prize, but it's the classic case of the tortoise and the hare.

Here are individuals who value respect; they do not want to be disrespected by anyone and will make sure they're not. Also, they will not disrespect another human being, which is a wonderful quality. They are demanding, but they are honest and thoughtful, and they won't expect anything of you that they haven't already tackled themselves.

Earth in Cancer needs to learn that life is serious, but it doesn't have to be a grind. It can be fun! Exercising their storytelling skills and wit is a highlight for this person—and for those around them. However, they hate to waste time and begin to feel guilty if they're having too much fun; they have a real need to put their talents to work to help those less fortunate.

The element of water is a blessing for Earth in Cancer people. They can be a little dry (physically as well as mentally), and simple things like drinking enough water, swimming, or walking in the rain, are very therapeutic. They are psychically attuned to Mother Earth, particularly to her seas and oceans. At some point, the enlightened Earth in Cancer may work in environmental ways for the seas, or the mammals, fish, and other creatures that are part of this wonderful psychic power of Mother Earth.

The aware Earth in Cancer is also here to develop their psychic natures. They are fascinated by the non-tangible realms and psychic abilities, but often find it difficult to trust their own intuitive impulses. Trust is a big issue for Earth in Cancer, but the more they do this, the more their uncanny intuitive abilities will be revealed. Through developing psychically, they realize the richness of life: that there is far more to it than just what we see and experience on the physical realm. This realization is especially important for Earth in Cancer because they have the potential to achieve goals both on the physical plane and on the spiritual realms of Earth. The enlightened Earth in Cancer has a strong desire to evolve and gain initiations on the spiritual planes.

One lesson for these individuals that will keep repeating is the balance between career and home life. At heart, they crave success in the outside world and can rise to the top of their profession through their disciplined approach and fine intelligence. However, it's as if they are constantly called back from the mountaintop to the vulnerable places of their own hearts through loved ones, friends, and family. They think they can exist on their own, but there is a yearning for closeness that is a lifelong lesson for this sign.

It's vitally important for them to have lofty goals throughout their lives, but equally as important to spend quiet times in nature or with those closest to them. This will replenish and rejuvenate them.

While others are becoming older and duller and set in their ways, Earth in Cancer begins to look younger and fresher than she did when she was thirty. This combination of Cancer and Capricorn is built to last with the correct healthy disciplines of body, mind, and spirit. Sometimes, though, she just won't feel like being disciplined—and why should she when she's vacationing in Sicily and enjoying the pasta and wine? She then happily enjoys herself without anxiety, until later when the discipline kicks back in and she is as good as new again. This sensible behavior is a balanced way of life and one that works for this combination.

Here is a sign that is learning to value others and also themselves. After a lot of deep thought, learning, and growth, they are ready to take on the world and know their own worth. The kind, caring, nurturing exterior can deflect you from the steely confidence within.

Let me give you an example of a typical Earth in Cancer person. She was one of my first editors. I remember when I met her I felt really pleased that she was such an easy-going, pleasant, and reserved personality. I felt that she would love my book and, apart from some expected edits, would keep everything as I wanted. The book was returned to me unrecognizable. It was full of edits but they weren't just regular edits, they were precise instructions (as opposed to suggestions) that I was supposed to follow to the letter. At first I argued with her then, when that didn't work, I reasoned with her and then, finally, I ended our telephone call and sulked for a day or two.

She had torn my book to pieces and now wanted me to put it together again. What nerve! What was she trying to do with my masterpiece? During my self-imposed sulking period, I realized I had no choice but to telephone her again. She was so gracious and delighted to hear from me. She was just as pleasant and respectful as ever. However, she hadn't budged an inch. What did I do? I had no choice but to obey—a horrible plight for my wayward Sun in Aries nature.

I swallowed my ego and followed every single instruction. The miraculous thing was that when I had finished, my book was far superior to my original version. Yes, I have to admit the aware Earth in Cancer has an uncanny intuition that just knows what's good and will do her best to help create masterpieces wherever she goes. Don't be fooled by appearances. This is a clever person who doesn't wear her heart on her sleeve, and so what you see is not always what you get!

It is also essential for Earth in Cancer to develop their feeling nature through regular spiritual practices such as prayer, healing, and meditation work. The extreme sensitivity of their psychic and spiritual nature is then allowed expression, bringing them fulfillment and inner joy. Their compassionate natures inspire them to help others wherever they go, and they do so with grand and generous gestures.

Earth in Leo/Sun in Aquarius

A person born with The Earth in Leo has the Sun in the opposite sign of Aquarius. These are both masculine fixed signs, and this combination is all about steadfastness and loyalty. Earth in Leo is a fixed Fire sign and Sun in Aquarius is a fixed Air sign. This combination brings honesty, independence, tolerance, idealism, generosity, strength, and humanitarianism. The enlightened Earth in Leo person is friendly, respectful, loyal, and understands equality, brotherhood, and Oneness—not just as idealistic concepts, but as powerful ways to bring positive change to our world.

With his Sun in unconventional Aquarius, the person with Earth in Leo tells it as he sees it and, because of this and other unusual traits, he is often misunderstood. He is inventive, telepathic, and unique.

Like all the Signs, Earth in Leo is not perfect. He's not as good at receiving advice as he is at dishing it out. He loves to stir the pot and ruffle other people's feathers, but doesn't enjoy conflict himself. Here is a person who would rather lead than follow because he thinks he knows best. Dogmatic and opinionated, it's hard for him to listen. Despite his rather contrary nature, he has a quiet side and often prefers to take a back seat so that he can "do his thing" uninterrupted and without disturbance. However, once he begins to draw on the vitality and magnetism of his Earth in Leo, he begins to shine, drawing people to him. Because this person has the courage to be exactly who he is, not caring too much about what other people think, he may often find himself in leadership positions whether he seeks them or not.

The lesson of the awakened Earth in Leo is to take that courageous step into the limelight and embrace it, to be prepared to be noticed because he can achieve a lot more here than when he fades into the background. It is here that he can begin to realize his potential. Earth in Leo needs to be seen, noticed, and admired because he is born to shine. One challenge, however, for this combination is the ego, and it is this that may keep him away from taking center stage. However, he is here to learn that, in order to express his full potential, he must learn how to use his ego in a positive way rather than just suppressing it. Self-mastery, rather than suppression of ego, is essential.

For example, this person has a unique way of looking at the world, and he thinks outside the box. He is intelligent and interested in the world and the people in it. He has a courageous mentality, a scientific mind, and he can grasp obscure topics. Because of this, he can use the positive aspects of his ego to teach or explain things to others in some way.

When you meet Earth in Leo for the first time, he may look at you with his faraway eyes, appearing to listen intently to every word with an enigmatic smile and making you feel like you're the most fascinating person in the world. What you probably don't realize is that he had swiftly analyzed you in the first five minutes of conversation, and already his mind is miles away on some distant planet.

Earth in Leo is a great friend to have when you're going through your own trials. The whole world can be against you, throwing accusations and nasty gossip at you but this person can ignore it all. He may listen with interest to what the others have to say, but it won't matter a jot to him because he made his mind up about you in that first five minutes and nothing is going to change that. There is something very liberating about that kind of friendship. Friendship, teamwork, and brotherhood are all concepts that he understands. Because of this, he enjoys a wide network of friends and acquaintances from all levels of society and in all parts of the world.

A big lesson though is learning to infuse the cool, detached, measured friendship of his Sun Sign in Aquarius, with the warmth of a loving heart. He can love the world in a detached way but, if he is to excel, he will also have to understand, love, and respect the person right in front of him. Earth in Leo is learning to demonstrate and express his feelings, appreciation, and admiration for others. He is learning that love without expression is meaningless. The more he does this, the more he will be using the potential of this warm and generous Earth sign.

As mentioned, both Leo and Aquarius are fixed signs that enjoy stability. However, this particular combination is one that experiences sudden changes. Others may think he is unstable, but in fact he needs to leave behind practical everyday concerns every now in order to recharge his batteries and be inspired by the lofty ideals that are a vital part of his life. When he does this, he will regain the stability that he needs for his health and happiness.

Earth in Leo is of the Fire element and if he is feeling down, he can literally stoke up the fires of his enthusiasm by basking in the Sun. If the Sun is not available, then it's very beneficial for him to have a fire—whether it is wood, gas, or electric does not matter. This will help to balance him and bring nourishment and warmth to the rarified nervous system of his opposite Sun in Aquarius.

Love is the fuel for us all, but especially for Earth in Leo—not just to receive it, but to learn to use it. This will ground him and help to open his heart more fully, and this is one of the biggest challenges for this analytical, scientific type of person. He should engage, on a regular basis, in spiritual disciplines such as prayer and healing, to express the warmth of his magnanimous heart.

It is also essential for this person to develop self-understanding, and he has to be prepared to turn the light of his intelligence on himself on a regular basis. Sometimes he may shock himself when he realizes he has a need for appreciation —which most of the time he hides away. In fact, it is far better for him to face this need, recognize it, and accept it.

The world needs great leaders; they are few and far between. His leadership style does not have to be aggressive or "in your face" quality; it's best for him to find his own unique style and follow that. Just think of Earth in Leo, Abraham Lincoln. He stepped into the limelight despite his awkward looks and manner, and decided anyway that he was going to become President. Despite numerous setbacks and failures and with great determination, he kept on going and eventually succeeded. What a wonderful leader he was!

Not everyone is here to become President of a country, or even a conventional leader. Earth in Leo is here to use his creativity to find a path that will fire up, uplift, and inspire him as well as others. It may be through teaching. Although not a natural teacher, he has such a unique manner that others are drawn to what he has to say. He can be extremely good with words, but may first have to learn how to express himself.

Learning how to teach, express, and communicate are important lessons for the person with Earth in Leo for, once he can do this, he can then explain the most complex subjects in the simplest way. Because he understands other people, he can speak in a way that reaches people. Once he develops true confidence, Earth in Leo can become quite an orator; he is able to sway people with his magnetic quality of mind.

The enlightened person with Earth in Leo and Sun in Aquarius is an "original," and his thinking is ahead of the masses, fifty years or more into the future. He is here to shock people out of their apathy, but must also be able to offer them something they can understand and enjoy. Instead of being regarded as quirky, Earth in Leo is here to develop such warmth and love of people that they will follow him even though they don't really understand where he or they are going. It takes courage to express the power of Earth in Leo, but then this combination can be courage personified.

Earth in Leo people are good parents but they are not exclusive, as they have a feeling of responsibility for all children. This is another aspect of their enlightened outlook, and having children or working with children is a grounding mechanism for

Earth in Leo. This person, seeking freedom for himself and his ideas, also abhors any system of indoctrination for others. He dislikes anything that belittles the human mind and spirit such as inequality, intolerance, prejudice, dishonesty, jealousy, bigotry, injustice, poverty, or war. Because of this, others see him as an idealist, espousing social causes for the betterment of the world. He is also a realist, who is prepared to turn his ideals into work, his desire for a better world into service—again, learning to express his warm and loving heart.

Earth in Leo with Sun in Aquarius is also a very creative combination. It is good for him to nurture and unlock the storehouse of his creativity. This can take many forms; it may be through writing, painting, cooking, designing, or inventing new ways of doing things. Somewhere in his life he needs to have a creative outlet for him to really shine.

With the awakened Earth in Leo, his spirituality is all embracing and cosmic. It is inclusive of all people, nature, plants, animals, the Earth, the Galaxy, all the planets, and more. He sees everything as an expression of the Divine, and a part of his expression is to inspire and be inspired. He is here to find meaningful ways to manifest his uniqueness and his clever mind.

This person has an innate and heartfelt understanding of the problems and sufferings of all people, as well as an appreciation for Mother Earth. He will never feel satisfied until he uses this global empathy in creative ways to help others. The more he evolves, the more his generous heart will lead him. There are many ways he will be called to serve. He is here to embrace these opportunities and not shrink from them, for he is here on Earth to shine and to inspire others to do the same.

Earth in Virgo/Sun in Pisces

A person born with The Earth in Virgo has the Sun in the opposite sign of Pisces. These are both feminine mutable signs, and this combination is adaptable and changeable in nature. Earth in Virgo is of the Earth element, and Sun in Pisces is of the Water element.

Earth in Virgo is naturally attuned to the mysterious and the spiritual due to having the Sun in dreamy, otherworldly Pisces. They often have strong psychic natures, and they can adapt to the changing flow of life; but their lifelong lesson is to ground their innate faith and devotion through acts of service. In other words, they are learning to apply their faith and to work hard in order to manifest their dreams.

Here is a person who doesn't naturally relate to the rigidity of time, but experiences it as a measurement of change, because his world is fluid and imbued with feelings. In the words of Albert Einstein, who had Earth in Virgo/Sun in Pisces, when he described his famous theory of relativity: *"When a man sits with a pretty girl for an hour, it seems like a minute. But let him sit on a hot stove for a minute – and it's longer than any hour. That's relativity."*

Because of the fluidity of their world, they are, therefore, often struggling to be on time and to master the basic, everyday things of the material world. When they consciously draw upon the power of Earth in Virgo, they can then add discipline to their everyday lives as well as to their spiritual lives, enabling them to cultivate depth, wisdom, and spiritual abilities.

People with the Sun in Pisces seek regular quiet downtime and peace, as this is helpful for them to achieve and maintain balance. They can snuggle up in bed with a good book or sleep at odd hours, but their opposite Earth in Virgo is calling for them to learn the lessons of productivity and consistency, as well as the basic, everyday things of life. The aware person realizes that too much peace is detrimental, so they strive to be as productive and consistent as possible. It is only then that they can be successful at achieving their goals and developing their skills.

It is hard to find a more patient and deeply empathetic person than the one who has this combination of Earth in Virgo/Sun in

Pisces. Here is a naturally non-judgmental person who can accept everyone as they are, with kindness and compassion. However, to manifest their fuller potential in this life, Earth in Virgo must develop their powers of discernment. If they don't, they can get pulled here and there by other people who would waste their time and suck their energy. If they don't, they can spend time seeking goals and ambitions that are doomed to end in failure without the structure of efficiency and consistency. They are here learning to create boundaries of time and energy in their lives. While they can still offer their loving natures to others who need help, they are learning to do so in ways that are more productive both to them and to the people they help.

It is essential for all of us, but particularly essential for the awakened Earth in Virgo individual, to have spiritual aims and goals. She can be completely dedicated and devoted as well as self-sacrificing and, because of this, she is capable of incredible deeds. However, she tends to be a dreamer and her constant challenge is to build structure so that she can live up to her deeper potential. It is helpful for this person to have a job or career that is geared to the service of others, for this will bring her the structure and sense of fulfillment that she needs.

So important is this to Earth in Virgo that, unless she learns to ground herself, through setting up lists, plans, and goals, she may find herself drifting and lost —half in this material world and half in the invisible realms of spirit. If this person feels lost, she can then fall prey to consciousness-numbing addictions. The aware person will soon realize that these do not bring the solutions that she needs. This person has a great need to have artistic and spiritual outlets in her life because she is creative, spiritually minded, and imaginative.

The awakened Earth in Virgo will turn to consciousness-enhancing practices such as meditation and spiritual practices more readily than most. However, the problem is that she can spend hours one day and then nothing for days on end. Until she sets up regular schedules and draws upon her practical power of the Earth in Virgo, the wonderful, blissful experiences she can achieve may be like a quick-fix sugar pill.

It is important for this combination of Earth in Virgo and Sun in Pisces to find balance between efficiency and consistency, and their aspirations and dreams. They should not allow practical concerns to stifle their dreams. To avoid this from happening, they should use their imaginations; they should seek solace in Nature and enjoy time meditating or contemplating for these types of activities will bring the inner peace, faith, and joy that they seek. The enlightened Earth in Virgo yearns for the joy that expanded consciousness brings, far more than having joy in a new car or other material object. They are here to seek the heightened consciousness where the birdsong is clearer, the Sun shines brighter, the flowers are even more brightly colored, and where the expressions of love, gratitude, and generosity, of which they are capable, make their hearts sing.

This is a person who doesn't like to be confined, but prefers to be free to swim with the tide of his imagination wherever that leads him. This is not a person to be cooped up in a strict and regimented corporate environment, who finds it hard to understand the linear structure of an 8 a.m. to 5 p.m. existence. If he is forced to do this type of work, his innate dedication will lead him to burn the midnight oil. He may come in late, but he will work in a dedicated way until the job is done. This is not a person who clock-watches, unless he is swimming in the wrong tide.

The more these individuals attune to the power of Earth in Virgo, the more they find themselves nudged back to a place of reality. While this is essential, they should also ensure they make time to express the magical part of who they are.

It is especially important for Earth in Virgo to find the right path—whether that it is their everyday job or their spiritual path. It's important they question their own motives from time to time. If they are in a job just to make money, they may find it difficult to remain motivated because money is not their key. They like to have money because it gives them the freedom they desire. They often seem to acquire it, but it doesn't really turn them on. While they need to pay the rent, they also need to be free to express their fine imagination and deeper yearnings through caring, charitable and spiritual channels.

Sometimes, Earth in Virgo people can appear to be in quite a meaningless routine, but if they love what they do—and love is the key for them—it really doesn't matter. I know a hospital administrator who has Earth in Virgo. She is really at home in this environment of healing and caring for the sick (this environment draws upon her practical Earth in Virgo energy as well as her opposite Pisces Sun energy and 'feeds' her in a positive way). Despite the number crunching involved in her work, she realizes that, through her sacrifice and surrender, she is contributing to the smooth running of the hospital and the care and healing of all the patients.

Occasionally, you will find Earth in Virgo to be an apparently hard-nosed character, for example, my dad. He was a tough undercover homicide detective all his working life, and yet he had his gentle, sensitive Sun in Pisces. He had a difficult upbringing and was a strong, realistic person. At first glance, he seemed nothing like a Pisces Sun. That's because he had, through life's experiences and a certain enlightened approach to life, learned to instinctively draw upon the power of his practical Earth in Virgo. However, the self-sacrifice, love, and desire to serve were always there deep down and very much a part of him. It was during my dad's career in homicide that he really found himself. The harsh nature of his job made him realize he could either become cynical or try to help the poor, downtrodden people he dealt with. He made a choice to take the higher path of sacrifice. One example of this was when he gave the kiss of life to a homeless person caked in dirt and grime whom the medics had said was dead—and he brought him back to life. In my dad's words, *"The man was reborn, and so was I. I suddenly realized why I was here."*

This is a pretty special person when awakened to the self-sacrificing nature of Love. Although I have stressed work, routine, and discipline for Earth in Virgo, actually this combination of Virgo and Pisces is all about love—love expressed through service to others. Love, in all its octaves, is their reality. Don't underestimate his non-judgmental trust and belief in other people. It may seem like weakness to you, but it is because he truly loves people, and this is his strength.

The enlightened Earth in Virgo person knows he can't judge others until he has walked a mile in their shoes. His lessons are to forgive, to understand, and to have faith. While the rest of the world may ignore the homeless man on the sidewalk begging for money or disdainfully throw him a handful of coins, the enlightened Earth in Virgo person not only smiles, stops for a chat, but also pays for lunch. With all the practicality of the Earth sign of Virgo, he knows that usually a smile is not enough! To Earth in Virgo, the homeless person is just as important as he is, and quite possibly more so. He may thank God that he is not in his shoes, but he will never condemn. He seems to know without ever being told that *"there but for the grace of God go I."*

These individuals are aware that their highest path is service, and that they are here to not just feel love for others, but to put this feeling of love into action. They instinctively know that the world is a terrible place not so much because of all the evil people in it, but more so because of the deadening apathy and lack of belief in miracles of the majority. Earth in Virgo/Sun in Pisces people are here to transmute apathy into loving service.

Their dedication and devotion to the Mother Earth is an integral part of the practical spirituality of the enlightened Earth in Virgo. They will find fulfillment in helping the environment through things like recycling. They will want to help preserve nature, trees, or endangered species. They will develop such a love and appreciation for our planetary home that they will want to begin their days with prayers of appreciation and gratitude for this wonderful living Intelligence. Through these regular rituals, they can truly ground their innate love of nature in ways that will not only bring transformation to our world, but the longed-for peace to their own sensitive natures.

Earth in Libra/Sun in Aries

A person born with The Earth in Libra has the Sun in the opposite sign of Aries. These are two masculine Cardinal signs, and this combination is action-oriented. Here is a person who doesn't just wait for opportunities, but likes to create them and get things done. Earth in Libra is a Cardinal Air sign, and Sun in Aries is a Cardinal Fire sign.

The constant challenge of Earth in Libra is to realize that they are not alone; that there is a world of people around them. As well as working hard to achieve their objectives, they should also take the time to form and nurture relationships and connections with other people. When they to do this, they can rise above the innate selfishness that they bring into this life to become one of the most giving and self-sacrificing of all the Signs.

Once Earth in Libra is inspired by an ideal, such as working for an environmental, charitable, or spiritual cause, he can become a true leader. When he joins his promotional talent with something bigger and nobler than himself, then he can become not only a leader—but an inspired leader. These people are easily recognized as leaders as they have a quiver of positive attributes—enthusiasm, dynamism, courage, loyalty, sincerity, and honesty—and they have the confidence in themselves to use these attributes to further their chosen cause.

Astrology books will tell you that the person with the Sun in Aries is selfish. However, this is not necessarily the case. Once he becomes conscious of the energy of Earth in Libra, he can give himself to a cause bigger and nobler than he is, more fully than almost any other sign. Don't forget this is a sign of courage; he is the person who, at his best, will risk his own life over and over again if necessary to pick you up from the battlefield of life and carry you to safety without a thought.

Learning moderation and balance will help this person to find his true center. He can go off, inspired and enthused by something, and just as quickly, lose interest and leave other people hanging. Once the battle is over and he's won, he doesn't dwell on the past, but moves on. This can be difficult for the more cautious souls to understand. Earth in Libra tends to live more fully in the moment than most other people—not thinking too much about the past or worrying about the future.

Once balance is learned and intelligently applied, this person can then function at his best. In fact, this person will never feel truly secure until he achieves some measure of equilibrium. This can be achieved through working in partnership or in relationships with like-minded people. When he does work with others for a common cause, he feels grounded and safe.

Another way to achieve balance is for Earth in Libra to look at himself honestly and fearlessly. It is beneficial for these people to study wisdom and spiritual texts, for this helps them realize that life does not revolve around them. They can also stay grounded by learning the art of gracious living—kindness, thoughtfulness, and honor—which can bring them the social advancement that they require to achieve their goals.

This combination of Earth in Libra/Sun in Aries is here to stir things up with energy and courageous actions, daring to go where no one has gone before. He is the pioneer who will be prepared to take a dangerous stance if necessary in order to achieve his noble objectives. However, he consciously needs to strive to embody the power of Earth in Libra to understand that he needs people on his side. Otherwise, he will find himself shouting in the dark with nobody listening, and this is not the way of a leader. This leader dares, but also negotiates with others.

This leader inspires by making connections and achieves through mediation and compromise. At his best, this is the type of leader who is a figurehead or spokesperson: a person who is a natural with public relations and relationships of all types.

This is not the person who should join the rank and file and refuse to make decisions or take any action until it is approved by the majority. It is not that at all. He takes his journey with other people but in some ways he is alone. More than others he knows that, at the end of the day, he can rely on nobody but himself. He knows that the place for him is out in front but to be most effective, he also has to learn to work with others. The good thing is that he can gather people around him with his charm and social grace.

This person is impulsive and his energy is like a flame, burning brightly with a creative thought or an idea. If his idea is strong and true, it can bring light to the darkest night. If his idea is strong and wild, it can cause devastation. Such is the power of the Libra Earth/Aries Sun combination. His goal is to introduce new ideas, thoughts, systems, and magic into our world. His mind works at warp speed, and he understood what you were trying to tell him from the first few seconds it was out of your mouth.

To make the most of his many talents, Earth in Libra should learn to stop and listen to others with full attention, even if he thinks he has all the answers. Often the reason he stops listening is not because he's rude, but because the impulse of his opposite sign of the Sun in Aries is always to remain first. In order to achieve this he knows he can't afford to waste time. He knows at some deep level that in some area of his life he must be his own boss, independent and free.

However, it is when he learns to give others the respect that he himself desires and craves, that he will be able to achieve his lofty goals more easily. While he is a great promoter of himself and his ideas, he can also be the best promoter of other people and causes he believes in if he is inspired by that person or cause. He is a good public speaker who can persuade and inspire others through his sheer passion, optimism, and enthusiasm for his subject.

This impulsive person may have many false starts and a good deal of wasted time until he learns to think before he acts; to discriminate on how best to use his energy and how to focus his mind, heart, and soul on what is truly important to him. For the spiritually minded person, his impulses—born from his higher nature—will lead him unerringly to where he is meant to be. If you have this combination, and right now find your life pretty well perfect with everything in place like a finished jigsaw puzzle, you can expect to find those intuitive impulses prompting you to move on!

This combination of Earth in Libra/Sun in Aries is possibly the most misunderstood of the zodiac because they operate best ahead of the crowd. Others may never be quite sure what they are up to. "What makes him tick?" "What are his motives?"

Being a masculine sign, the Aries women have an even harder time. *"Why does she have to be so aggressive?" "What is she trying to prove?" "What does he want out of life?"* She doesn't seem to care one hoot for money, often making a heap and then losing it all again with hardly a murmur.

She can rise to the heights of her profession quickly and capably, not caring one jot that it's supposed to be harder for a woman to reach the top. Then once she conquers these dizzy heights, she is likely to leave everything behind to bum around the world on a shoestring. Security, position, money, fear, guilt, politics, or popularity doesn't turn her on at all; challenge and all that is real and true does. Once you understand that, you begin to understand this person.

A person with the Earth in Libra and the Sun in Aries is born to be on the cutting edge. The life of a pioneer is never about comfort and security. When he follows his higher impulses and works hard to make things happen, when he listens to others with love and respect but still remains his own person with his own independent viewpoint, all his needs will be met. His lesson is to be considerate and respectful of others, to be open to their opinions, and also to have faith in himself and his own unique vision.

If you don't have that kind of faith, ask yourself: *"How can I learn to have that kind of faith? Where do I start?"* With this combination, it begins with self-knowledge, self-understanding, and being open to wise counsel from others whom he trusts.

You are fortunate if you have earned the respect of a friend with the Earth in Libra/Sun in Aries. He will fight for you when the world is against you; encourage you when you are down with his boundless energy and enthusiasm; believe in you and your dreams and refuse to acknowledge the bad things about you. In this way, he is an idealist. Once he believes in something, he will focus solely on the good. His passion is hot, strong, and burns brightly. His friends are few and far between; but once this person has a friend, he will battle with them and for them, through thick and thin. His friendships may be few, but his loyalty is immense.

His refreshingly simple, honest, direct, and frank approach to life may seem naïve to others. However, it is important he doesn't bury his head in the sand and remain unaware of the politics around him. For a true balanced approach, he will employ his Earth in Libra to understand the politics and gossip that abounds in every corner of life, to deal with them if necessary, to bring the light of truth and honesty, but never to attach to them. It's important for this person to avoid wasting his precious time in non-productive, negative ways. His purpose in life is achievement. It's easier for him to focus on the positive so he can achieve his goals without any distractions to pull him off course.

Many people strive to find peace, but Earth in Libra/Sun in

Aries is born to fight injustice where it exists. He knows that peace will not come while greed and selfishness prevail. He is here to fight every act of pettiness, jealousy, and anger that burns within every heart. There will come a day when he realizes his most challenging fight is to tame his own passionate nature: controlling his basic thoughts, emotions and actions.

The message for Earth in Libra/Sun in Aries is—believe in yourself, be true to yourself, and trust your impulses! Love yourself, and don't allow others less inspired to dampen your noble spirit. Be disciplined, but don't be too hard on yourself. Listen to the wise counsel of others whom you respect, and seek their help when needed. Seek freedom, action, and adventure; be courageous and always be geared towards helping others with your every thought and action—and the world will be your oyster!

Earth in Scorpio/Sun in Taurus

A person born with The Earth in Scorpio has the Sun in the opposite sign of Taurus. These are two feminine Fixed signs, and this combination is reliable and constant with a special affinity for Mother Earth. Earth in Scorpio is a Fixed Water sign, and Sun in Taurus is a Fixed Earth sign.

These people never want to be pushed. They have a lot of energy in reserve, and they are very aware of their boundaries. They do not want other people to cross these boundaries without permission. If their security is threatened in any way, they do not take kindly to this. In other words, this combination of Earth in Scorpio/Sun in Taurus is to alert to people and things that would intrude in their personal space. They are here learning to trust, and this lesson for them is often a lengthy process.

This is also a serious combination, not a lighthearted one, because this person can see the heights that can be reached, as well as the depths to which one can sink. Here is a person who often grapples with the spiritual side of her nature as well as the more basic aspects. However, once Sun in Taurus embraces the higher aspects of their Earth in Scorpio through self-knowledge and self-mastery, then there are no bounds to the heights to which this 'Eagle in the making' can fly.

The aware Earth in Scorpio persons seeks value and wants to do something worthwhile with their lives. When they find it, they can dive in with great passion and intensity of purpose. They do not naturally seek the limelight or a leadership role, but they do feel comfortable with power. They prefer to remain behind the scenes, for example, holding the reins of power through taking control of the flow of money.

This is a combination of great strength, persistence, and determination. Once things are set in motion, this person can, through sheer force of will, achieve her goals. However, the initial act of moving in this direction sometimes takes a while because here is a person who doesn't rush impulsively, but prefers to wait. She waits because she does not feel it is the right time to act, or because she is not yet equipped with enough resources. At times this can be an excuse to do nothing because, at heart, the opposite sign of Taurus yearns for a pleasant time. And for her, a pleasant time often means one where she is not disturbed too much, but can remain comfortably fixed in her routines and her opinions.

However, once this person awakens to the power of her Earth in Scorpio, she will then, with willpower and determination, move fearlessly and relentlessly towards her goals. The lifelong lesson for Earth in Scorpio is to avoid the comfortable rut.

What awakens and moves Earth in Scorpio people is the depth of their feelings. Despite the outer cool, calm mask they wear, they are, in fact, people of deep feelings and great sensitivity. They come alive with a breathtaking sunset or a beautiful view of Nature. They feel the pain of those who are sick and suffering. They feel appalled at the plight of Mother Earth as humanity continues to take all he can from Her in order to satisfy his own greed.

The awakened Earth in Scorpio cannot just ignore their deeper feelings. They recognize that these are promptings of their souls to move them in the right direction and embrace the opportunities and challenges ahead. They know they are here to add value and purpose to not just their own lives or to the lives of their families, but also to the lives of humanity as a whole. They are often very concerned about Mother Earth and Her resources with a deep affinity and love for this beautiful planet.

One fascination for Earth in Scorpio is money and usually at some point in their lives they will be dealing with financial matters, often handling other people's money. They are skillful in dealing with money because they understand that it is energy and, like all other energy, it can be controlled and used wisely. Their innate common sense helps them to thrive and succeed in careers such as banking, insurance, and anything that involves persistence, stability, and relentless drive. They can then use their financial resources to build or support a worthy charity or venture, for it is their innate desire to build something of value that really moves and inspires them.

To the enlightened Earth in Scorpio, it is not so much the money itself that they cherish, it's everything of substance in life; everything that adds value and purpose to life. This may be a close friendship, or their cherished ideals for a better world.

Earth in Scorpio person is strength personified, and she has a great deal of physical magnetism and innate vitality that can heal and uplift those around her. While every person has the capacity to heal others, the combination of strength and deep feelings of Earth in Scorpio has the potential to be an especially magnetic and exceptionally gifted healer. Healing is a wonderful way for them to channel their natural vitality in a way that will not only help others, but also help them to control their own deep moods and emotions.

This person can be very charming indeed; but with her sensitivity and hidden depths, it is usually best to avoid direct, off-the-cuff, lighthearted remarks aimed in her direction. You may only be joking, but Earth in Scorpio takes things to heart and needs time to assimilate and mull things over. She is constantly seeking the truth in any experience but the truth can be painful for this strong, but extremely sensitive person.

Earth in Scorpio is all about control and, like the sign of Aries, she's proud of her strength and doesn't need to be reminded that women are equal to men. This is a real woman who understands and uses her feminine nature. An enlightened female Earth in Scorpio is not afraid to use her wiles to get what she wants, as long as she feels that her battle is worth fighting. Earth in Scorpio is a real man with a romantic heart and sweetness of soul, but not one who can be easily manipulated or pushed in any way.

Here is a person, male or female, who is prepared to fight to make a difference with important issues concerning Mother Earth or environmental issues in the highest political circles if necessary. She has a commonsense way of speaking that reaches the heart of a problem, and the hearts of others. She is able to make the most complex and abstract ideals concrete. However, this person soon learns that not everyone has her desire for direct speaking, and it behooves her to apply the intelligence and perception of Earth in Scorpio and learn a certain political adroitness. This, combined with her strength and determination, can bring the results she desires.

Another word associated with this combination is security. It's not just that she seeks this, but also that she brings it. Earth in Scorpio will definitely ruffle your feathers from time to time but despite that you will feel secure around her. Her friends, and even strangers, feel that here is a solid, dependable, person that they can rely upon. This is especially noticeable during times of crisis. Earth in Scorpio is able to draw on a deep inner strength that enables her to remain cool, calm, and collected—especially when those around her are floundering, fearful, and unsettled.

While Sun in Taurus people are firmly grounded on this physical plane of Earth, once they awaken more fully awaken to the power of their Earth in Scorpio, they begin to seek things of a non-physical, subtle nature. They seek meaning, fulfillment, and knowledge of the invisible worlds. While they are not easily fooled and demand proof and evidence, more and more they yearn to understand the ancient mysteries and other magical things, such as life after death, the purpose of life, and their own Spiritual natures that they increasingly cannot deny.

Earth in Scorpio takes things that she values very seriously. This may be making money, performing voluntary work, or creating relationships. As far as relationships are concerned, it may take her several years before she decides you're the one. Once she does, however, you have little say in the matter. You will be drawn into the magical web she weaves like a fly to a spider's web. The difference is you will enjoy the experience!

Earth in Scorpio people usually have more than enough cash in their pockets (they prefer the feel and substance of cash), but they don't like to make money by slaving over a computer or being cooped up in an office all day. Although they can work extremely hard, they prefer to *attract* money and opportunities to themselves and usually succeed. Once they have built up a business, which is often connected with land and real estate, they will then sell it and begin all over again. Generally, they are not interested in the day-to-day, nitty-gritty of running a business; they are more interested in creating something from nothing— building, rebuilding, and making money.

The person with the Sun in Taurus/Earth in Scorpio can endure routine work as long as the result is useful and valuable. However, the enlightened Earth in Scorpio has to beware of becoming so stuck in a rut for the sake of peace and security that he does not express his potential. He needs to find something of value that will fire his passion at a high level; something that will awaken his soul's desires.

While he needs to be rooted in reality, he also needs excitement, passion, and intensity. He values things that are strong and solid, concrete, and tangible. Not for Earth in Scorpio vague dreams and promises, ideas and ideals: he enjoys building things and seeing the results of his efforts. He is good at maintaining, sustaining, and perfecting what others have already started and does this in a responsible way. If he feels something is worthwhile, he is prepared to work long and hard with quiet persistence and determination; not giving up until he achieves the results he desires. The awakened Earth in Scorpio can overcome obstacles and opposition without blinking an eyelid or shedding a tear.

Earth in Scorpio has a generous heart and, although she is not easily moved to tears by the plight of the world, she is prepared to roll up her sleeves and work hard to help those less fortunate. Her vision of beauty, comfort, and safety is not just for herself, but for everyone in the world; and she is here to play her part to make this happen.

She has a highly attuned value system; and, as a grounded person of discernment and common sense, she values practical, useful things that add richness, beauty, comfort, and spirituality to life. Her life revolves around seeking out principles, things, and people of value and incorporating them into her life.

The evolved Earth in Scorpio is a person of great principle who has old-fashioned, enduring values. In a world of quick fixes and me-first mentality, this person is ethical and seeks integrity before superficial pleasures; she values honor, candor, and honesty above a clever tongue; common sense and wisdom above intellect.

Her opposite Sun in Taurus has, as a co-ruler, the planet Earth, and so there is a natural affinity to Mother Earth. The awakened Earth in Scorpio will want to give back to the Earth in some way and may be inspired to discover some of the sacred secrets of the Earth's ancient mysteries.

Earth in Sagittarius/Sun in Gemini

A person born with the Earth in Sagittarius has the Sun in the opposite sign of Gemini. These are two masculine Mutable signs, and this combination is about movement and flexibility. Earth in Sagittarius is a Mutable Fire sign, and Sun in Gemini is a Mutable Air sign.

The person with the Earth in Sagittarius and the Sun in Gemini has a lightness of step and mental acuity; he lives in the present moment and is the communicator and the teacher of the zodiac. One minute you see him, the next minute he is gone. His energy is like static electricity—constantly active and bouncing from one place to another. He is a good companion, quick-witted, playful, and fun. He is intelligent, articulate, versatile, inquisitive, shrewd, and congenial. He has the ability to see many sides. This can make him appear superficial, but in fact he is just examining all possibilities, and it can be hard for him to make a definite decision. He understands that the only constant in life is change.

This combination is rather like the wind. You don't know when the wind is coming, and when it comes, you can't tell how long it will blow before it changes directions, speed, or intensity. Sometimes it's a welcome breeze on a warm day, and other times an unwelcome hurricane that knocks your house down. Most of the time, it's something you may not even notice, but it's always there in the background gently moving things around, rustling the branches of the trees, kicking up the dust at times—but most of the time, welcome. When it stops, you surely miss it! Things seem dull and flat when the wind stops. When this person is around, he has a way of livening things up, and when he leaves, things usually wind down.

This person is interested in all knowledge, and this can lead him in diverse and scattered directions in which he becomes 'Jack of all trades and master of none.' In order to feel grounded, the overriding need is for this person to embrace the power of his

Earth in Sagittarius to ground his energies and find balance. Until he does this, he will be pulled here and there as he tries the myriad of tempting paths that are constantly presented to him. To find the right path, he has to dig deep beyond his clever intellect to the intuition of his Earth in Sagittarius. To first trust his own intuition, he will try many different spiritual practices until he finds the ones that will work for him and lead him on a higher path.

There is a tendency with this combination to find what he believes is his path and then dogmatically to believe it is the *only* path. To remain grounded, he should be open to others, to listen to others' commonsense and wisdom and to realize that he may have a *part of the truth*—but that there is always more.

Underneath his quick mind and gift of gab, Earth in Sagittarius is a true seeker of knowledge. Until he has gained a certain degree of awareness, he will want to lecture others, using ten words (where one would do). He wants to be known as the one who knows everything, or as others may say 'the know-it-all.' He has a little bit of knowledge here and a little bit there, but he will only be grounded once he decides which subject to learn about in-depth, i.e., which path to take. His path may be a spiritual path, a path of service, or of higher learning.

Until this person awakens to the power of his Earth in Sagittarius, he is so dazzled by the multitude of paths and opportunities that he may travel the world to find the path for him. Until this person finds his Path (with a capital "P"), he may feel lost or unfocused; never really feeling settled enough to achieve what he was born to do.

To be truly successful in his desire to expand the horizons of his life and yet not lose focus, this person should embrace the higher path that Earth in Sagittarius brings. Then he can explore fearlessly with an open heart and mind and inspire confidence in others through teaching and living his beliefs. When he coura-geously takes to the path of Truth offered by his Earth in

Sagittarius, he will gain a certain peace and balance, as well as the enthusiasm, joy, and sense of fun that is his birthright.

When this person awakens to his potential, he will find a desire to listen as well as teach, to understand, as well as to lecture. He is then well on the way towards becoming a wise teacher who thinks globally, while at the same time helping other people to find their paths in life, thus expanding the horizons of his own and others' lives.

The awakened Earth in Sagittarius needs to feel that he is moving, growing, and evolving, not stuck in one place—whether that place is a physical, mental, or spiritual. Ever wishing to move forward, he may seek the path of higher education to further broaden his mind; or travel, so that he can learn about different cultures and integrate what he has learned into his life. He does not travel aimlessly, but does so in order to understand the world and the people in it and to find a spiritual philosophy that makes sense of it all.

Another way for the person with Earth in Sagittarius to ground himself is through the element of Fire, which is Sagittarius' natural element. This can be the fire of the Sun, or a crackling fireside. In the awakened person, the Spiritual fire blazes forth illumination and inspiration. Then he is no longer just the wind in the background, but a person who injects passion, enthusiasm, and vitality into life. At this point, people really sit up and take notice.

The awakened Earth in Sagittarius person, once he finds his Spiritual Path, has an inspirational quality. He seems to be able to pluck ideas out of the ethers around him and forge them into a futuristic vision. Once he is able to do this, he can then aspire to true leadership.

Even once the Path is found, this will always be a changeable, mutable sign containing the duality of the opposite Sun in Gemini. Because of this inherent flexibility, he gets on well with both sexes and is open to many different points of view. He is often slim in build; it's all the constant movement and a desire to be light on his feet and ready for flight at any time that keeps him lean and lithe. The women are the same, and although feminine, they are often tomboys, such as a modern day Audrey Hepburn. This innate duality impacts everything they do.

Life is not measured in hours and minutes for this fascinating person, but rather in experiences. If he meets an old friend along the way, he may stop for a coffee and chat and then decide to buy a couple of books at the local bookstore and, in no time at all, the day has gone. He may not have achieved what he set out to achieve, but Earth in Sagittarius will have found richness in the experience that he can learn from in some way. Even if he's gone a few hours, it's doubtful that anyone will have to worry where he is because he'll be well armed with the latest technical gadgets. He does well in this computer age when everything is fast and instantaneous, and he enjoys being on the cutting edge.

This person is a lover of freedom who needs plenty of space. The awakened soul will at some point offer himself and his energies to help bring this same prized freedom to others who do not have it. The ruling planet of Sagittarius is Jupiter, but the co-ruler is the Earth. With this strong connection with Mother Earth, here is a person who can use his intelligence and wisdom to be a part of an innovative solution for humanity's future upon this beautiful planet. Much is demanded of Earth in Sagittarius for him to live the high ideals offered by his ruling planets. If he is not adhering to these high ideals, this person may feel something missing in his life.

Almost more than any other combination, this person must seek peace within on a regular basis. When he does this, he will be guided and helped on his journey by signs along the way, and by his own higher self.

The person with Earth in Sagittarius is proud of his intellect, but when he meets his intellectual superior, another scenario may ensue. The enlightened soul will not hesitate to adopt the superior as an adviser, teacher, guru, or mentor and have great respect for one of the few people from whom he feels he can learn. Other people may not have the humility to drop their own ideas in favor of others even though they may apparently be more enlightened. A more basic person will feel threatened by the superior intellect and wisdom and may strike out with sarcasm or shut down the conversation and be gone. However, the awakened Earth in Sagittarius has Truth as his prize; and as soon as he senses that another has more truth than he does, he will not hesitate to change in light of this.

Another thing that truly grounds Earth in Sagittarius is living fully in the moment, in the light of a bigger picture than a purely personal life. Once he has found the life philosophy or Spiritual Path that he seeks, he can then stop wishing for what could be or what might be, and fully immerse himself in life. This brings him greater vitality and enthusiasm even for those repetitive everyday things, for it is as if he is now seeing things for the first time.

Finally, Earth in Sagittarius is a mediator between heaven and earth, intuition and reason, wisdom and knowledge. He is, like the opposite Sun in Gemini, the interpreter as well as the messenger. The enlightened person is here to spread the message of his vision for Mother Earth. He is here to teach others how to care for Her and explain to them why they should. His message is broad for all humanity, for he has the ability to distil his knowledge in a way that everyone can understand. He is the messenger who is here to deliver the truth, irrespective of how it is received by others. He is here to pass on knowledge and to provide solutions to problems, bringing light and wisdom into the world.

Earth in Capricorn/Sun in Cancer

A person born with the Earth in Capricorn has the Sun in the opposite sign of Cancer. These are two feminine Cardinal signs, and this combination is about action and activity. Earth in Capricorn is a Cardinal Earth sign, and Sun in Cancer is a Cardinal Water sign.

The person with the Earth in Capricorn and the Sun in Cancer has a strong nurturing nature. The enlightened person is like a mother or father for all life—human, animal, and plant—who strives to bring their dreams for a better world into manifestation. For this person to succeed, she must understand and draw upon the power of Earth in Capricorn. If she does this, she can then build the plans and structures necessary for her dreams to take root and manifest.

This combination is not here to invent something new, but rather to take the best of what has been achieved before her and make it even better. This person is drawn to traditions; she honors and upholds these, for she understands that the best traditions are the foundations of life. She also understands the nature of power, how to embrace power, and use it wisely. Here is a person who has leadership potential—who could be the head of an environmental organization, charity, or spiritual organization. It is important for this person to spend her time and energy in meaningful and fulfilling pursuits, as this will satisfy her warm and caring natures.

However, if these people refuse to awaken to the potential of their Earth in Capricorn, they may shy away from their real source of power, preferring to immerse themselves in a purely personal life of friends and family. If they do this, they will never achieve the heights of which they are capable—for they are here not just for their families, but for the family of humanity. They are here to open their loving hearts to all, and they express this through their actions.

Individuals with the Earth in Capricorn and Sun in Cancer have a strong, active, psychic nature, and they *feel* their way through life to find what they are seeking. They have strong intuitive powers that will protect them from taking the wrong path if they are alert to these feelings. However, Earth in Capricorn needs to not just feel, but also to think things through, strategize, and plan, based on these feelings. If they do this, they have the power to reach the heights of their noble ambitions.

When Earth in Capricorn finds a cause or a career of quality that will fulfill their aspirations, they can then pour themselves into it, working long hours to achieve their objectives. When awakened to their true potential, they have great strength, maturity and wisdom, and seem almost invincible to other lesser mortals. They are able to do whatever it takes, shouldering great responsibilities, and meeting any challenge they face with determination to succeed.

At times, the responsibilities they have taken on may feel like a burden to this caring, sensitive person—they may literally feel the weight of the world on them. It is then vitally important for them to also nurture themselves. It is important for them to spend quiet time with those close to them, enjoying the fruits of Mother Earth, spending time in peaceful surroundings so that they can retreat and recharge their batteries so that they are strengthened and prepared to continue their work.

This person is not so much linear, but fluidic in nature, seeking form. The grounding of Earth in Capricorn comes from bringing the subtleties of moods, energy flows, and the constant flux of life into the form of a wise, mature person. This person can reach inwards to her psychic and spiritual natures and then reach outwards, empowered and strengthened, to help transform the world through her achievements.

The awakened Earth in Capricorn is an important person in these challenging days, ruled as they are by the Planet Saturn. Their strength is that of their natural element, water. Flowing water appears gentle and soft, but over time, it has the power to break rocks into sand. Its tides may not be seen on the surface, but once you enter the water, you can feel its strength. This inner strength of Earth in Capricorn comes from the spiritual and psychic power inherent within this person's nature and strong will.

There is yet another side of this complex personality. For this person, self-preservation is paramount. It is important to understand the source of his deepest needs and his darkest moods. When he feels challenged, his self-preservation instincts step in. With his Sun in Cancer, the security needs of himself and his family are of prime importance, and these are the foundation of his being. If you mess with these, you may feel the full force of this emotionally powerful person in a way that you will never forget—and neither will he.

However, when he draws upon the power of his opposite Earth in Capricorn, this person transforms into a wise, mature, balanced, grounded person who responds with logic, grace, and decisiveness. Here is a person who, because of his psychic sensitivity, can sense the motives of the other person and respond accordingly. Of course, if the other person truly is trying to hurt him or someone else, he has the courage to respond accordingly, and then the full force of this person of action and refined emotions will be seen and admired. Earth in Capricorn/Sun in Cancer is a combination never to underestimate.

While Earth in Capricorn do not usually seek the limelight; being a Cardinal sign such as Aries and Libra, they are pretty good at "getting it," through promoting themselves and the causes and projects with which they are involved. When they draw upon this practical, solid, wise part of their natures, they can set practical goals whereby they can manifest their dreams, and they can achieve them in a way that is enjoyable.

There is another positive attribute of this combination: when you first meet Earth in Capricorn/Sun in Cancer, you feel they are fully engaged and that this interaction with you is the most important thing going on. While other people may be distracted, this combination likes to stay in the here and now, centered in what is happening between him and the other person, people, animal, or plant.

By now, you might have the impression that this is the most perfect combination of all. As warm, caring people, they are among the best; but there is definitely a downside to all this subjective, sensitive humanness. Because this person is so concerned and intimately wrapped up with everything and everybody, he can suffer from excessive anxiety, with a desire to control his life and the lives of those close to him. When things don't go his way, and his close friends and family members don't go along with him, he can be upset. While a tougher, more abrasive soul takes disagreement and even insults in his stride, it may deeply wound this more sensitive person. Unless he has something tougher such as an Aries Moon or Sagittarius Ascendant, he may take upsets as a personal affront, and it could take days to prize him out of his melancholy when he's upset. Not that he's weak, he's as strong-willed as anyone and tenacious to boot—just highly sensitive.

Also, with his emotional nature, he feels and fears things other people don't even notice. He can be shy with strangers and difficult to get close to. He finds it difficult to trust people, and even the slightest hint of a threat can make him retreat into a dark place that he inhabits until his next mood-change. This could take place in the next few minutes, or it may take a few days, depending on the level of upset or his mood swings. At least he keeps life interesting, if not a little chaotic for the more orderly types, such as Virgo or Capricorn.

However, when this person draws upon the more pragmatic side of his Earth in Capricorn, he is able to control his sensitive nature and look objectively at things and people in a realistic way. He is then able to see things clearly as they really are, not through the lens of his emotional nature. Detachment is another gift that Earth in Capricorn brings, and this is the key to success in all his achievements.

Another lesser known thing about Earth in Capricorn is that

he is a wonderful storyteller. This is because he remembers everything that has happened in his life in vivid and sometimes gory detail (remember, every experience to him is an "encounter" and it impresses itself on his emotions). He remembers things from his childhood, your childhood, and in some cases from past lives too! As well as that, he is a good actor with expressive features and a wide range of emotions. In his storytelling, which can be verbal and in writing, he draws on his rich emotions and can make his audience laugh, weep, as well as feel inspired, depressed, or joyful, all in the space of a few minutes. He is also a brilliant mimic, with his keen eye for people's behavior and quirky characteristics. He is able to hold onto things, and through this acquisitiveness, he can also hold onto other people's attention.

However, unless he draws upon his innate desire for perfection that comes from utilizing the power of Earth in Capricorn, his talents may come to nothing much. He is not pushy, as some other signs may be, but he gets where he wants, just through keeping on, one step after the other. Earth in Capricorn is determined, strong-willed, and just as the mountain goat, he will reach his goals by putting one sure foot in front of the other.

This person, though intuitive, needs to temper his emotions and gut feelings with the realism of Earth in Capricorn. Suddenly, his strong feelings will have form. From that point onward, he can translate his desires for a better world into powerful actions. This person loves to dream and has a vivid imagination—but it is only when his dreams are combined with works that he can succeed.

The awakened Earth in Capricorn person is driven by a need to protect not only their families and friends, but also humanity as a whole and the precious Mother Earth.

Earth in Aquarius/Sun in Leo

A person born with the Earth in Aquarius has the Sun in the opposite sign of Leo. These are two masculine Fixed signs, and this combination is about strength and reliability. Earth in Aquarius is a Fixed sign of the Air element, and Sun in Leo is a Fixed Fire sign. Positive characteristics include generosity, magnanimity, confidence, vitality, enthusiasm, and vision.

The person with the Earth in Aquarius and the Sun in Leo is learning to balance the need for praise and attention with the desire to give praise and attention to others.

Think of how the Sun warms the Earth and how people, animals, and flowers come out and bathe in its life-giving rays when it shines. Sun in Leo people are rather like this with their sunny dispositions and warm, personable personalities. People are drawn to their magnetism, which is so tangible it literally warms you and draws you into their orbit. This is good for the Leo person because he loves to have an appreciative audience. He has a big heart and a generous, giving nature; and he has the ability to lead and inspire.

You won't have to look very far to spot this person. He is usually up in front of the crowd making a lot of noise, or otherwise attracting attention. Because of his lack of shyness, you may find him on stage acting or speaking, or leading a company or organization. He knows his place is center stage, and this strong sense of self is tempered when he draws upon the opposite—Earth in Aquarius.

To avoid the excessive egotism that Sun in Leo can bring and to center himself, he should draw on the power of his Earth in Aquarius. This combination of Aquarius and Leo is detached enough from the applause of others to no longer need or require it. While he still enjoys the limelight, it is no longer essential to his happiness and fulfillment. Now, he can become a true leader who understands people and pours his generosity and creativity on others; helping them to shine as he does, and helping them to be the best they possibly can be.

These people have a knack for knowing who is good at what. They have the generosity of spirit to empower others. They know the strengths of other people and will openly admire and applaud them.

The awakened person with the Earth in Aquarius is at his best when making decisions, taking responsibility, facing challenges courageously, protecting others without thought of himself, and generous to a fault. This person is strong, magnetic, and vital. He has a strong constitution and often has excellent health and recuperative powers.

There are, however, a few downsides, even with this sparkling soul, especially if you disrespect him. The Achilles heel of this combination is a tremendous pride that makes him vulnerable to slights, and he is easily wounded. He can roar so loudly that children and dogs run like the wind, but try roaring back and he is off. He demands respect, and he is deeply hurt if you ignore him.

When he uses his intelligence rather than his emotions to respond to others, he then becomes fascinated by what makes people tick; and when he does that, he can become one of the best leaders. He can, with his clever style of inspiring others, enthuse them into espousing a Cause that is dear to his heart; one that he knows is important, such as the future of the planet upon which we live.

With Earth in Aquarius and Sun in Leo, this person is particularly self-conscious and aware. Although he may appear laid-back in the extreme, he is actually coiled and ready to pounce. His laid-back, cool look is not just to impress, but it hides an inner intensity. Here is a proud person who doesn't want others to see his more vulnerable human side. In fact, he rarely acknowledges it himself, because his main focus is a creative, extrovert one, rather than an inward-looking one.

This person understands the saying, *"Play up, play up, and play the game"* because he knows that life is a game, and we are all actors on the stage of life. Because he understands this, he is usually very successful in life. He is ambitious and clever, and he exudes an air of authority. He also understands the power of delegation, especially those little, dull, or messy tasks. He knows that his role is to lead and inspire, so he can happily delegate the details. Because he is able to see the whole, rather than become caught up in the details, he is very good at setting up efficient, streamlined systems for others to use.

The person with Earth in Aquarius likes to appear confident and at ease, but he can actually be very humble. How can that be? Surely, he is the arrogant, confident one; but where does humility factor into this? It is sometimes difficult to see at first glance, but first, one must understand this person's innate sense of responsibility. He wants to be in control and is happy when others lean on him (he certainly doesn't want to lean on anyone else). If anything goes wrong in his life, rather than blaming anyone else, he will take the blame himself. The more evolved Aquarius/Leo is then, instead of being vain and self-absorbed, he is self-aware. This, combined with the intelligence to put things into perspective, brings the humility that is apparent when this person moves from ego to a more aware and enlightened way of being. You may not read that in astrology books, but it is true.

When this person embraces the power of his Earth in Aquarius, you have a person who wants to make a difference, one who has a need to shine light and love on the darkness of our world. The enlightened Earth in Aquarius person is not just concerned with his own purely personal world, but he is also concerned with the whole of humanity. When he has achieved his own personal ambitions, his next step will be to set up charitable foundations for the good of others. Don't be surprised if this person is motivated by providing food and education for thousands and millions of people around the world.

The person with the Earth in Aquarius and Sun in Leo thinks

big, and he has the intelligence and vision to make his dreams for a better world a reality. It is then that he feels really good about himself. Now, the kingdom of Sun in Leo can expand—Aquarius style, to half the civilized world!

While not everyone with Earth in Aquarius can make such a bold difference to our world, deep down within them all is a desire to do so: to light up the darkness and bring peace to chaos. This is because they have extremely generous hearts, and they respond to the needs of those less fortunate than themselves.

When this combination is out of balance, focusing solely on their Sun in Leo, they can be jealous, especially in matters of the heart; but when they draw on their Earth in Aquarius, they just cannot and will not indulge in petty emotions. This just does not suit Aquarius, whose ideals are far too noble and far-reaching to be overly concerned about emotional issues for very long. They are quite capable of plucking out the cause of jealousy from their lives by ending the relationship causing the trouble in a very detached way.

This combination has an affinity with children, and his tendency towards arrogance is more than compensated for by his generous displays of fun, love, and magnanimity all rolled into one. This enlightened soul is into joy and creativity just as a child, and a certain childlike vulnerability and trust remains with him throughout his life. He usually gets his heart broken more than once because of this, but few will even know about it. As babies, they are love bugs; they coo and smile; they are pretty and gorgeous; everyone makes a fuss about them and gives them all the love they want and need. The Leo baby can become so used to adoration, unquestioning loyalty, and support that he grows up thinking the world is his oyster. And usually it is.

Because this person is usually so much larger than life, he can attract jealousy from other smaller-minded souls who want to take him down a peg or two. However, with his philosophical nature, he is able to take it in his stride and carry on, hurting inside, but you would never know it. With his superior manner, he refuses to go down to the level of other lesser souls!

As well as being hugely creative and able to fix things or turn a block of wood into a work of art in almost any realm of endeavor, from a failing business to a blank canvas, Earth in Aquarius also makes for the best hosts who can turn any dinner party into a glitzy Hollywood affair!

Love is a big thing for this combination. The Sun in Leo is a romantic soul who understands the romance of love affairs; and when they embrace their Earth in Aquarius, they are extremely loyal, accepting, and understanding of their partner's faults and idiosyncrasies.

One thing though, they cannot tolerate being ignored, being unappreciated, or being taken for granted. You may say "who does?" But for this combination, it is a more of a necessity.

This person wants to love people; this is his natural state. He can forgive and rise above pettiness or nastiness. He respects everyone, no matter what their position, status, age, color, creed, or nationality. For the evolved Earth in Aquarius, these values form the basis of his life.

As a person concerned with society and the whole of humanity, he is also concerned deeply about the planet Earth upon which we live. At some point in his life, he will devote his time, resources, and love, to the beautiful Mother Earth. Earth in Aquarius is too intelligent to think that we can continue as we are, reaping everything we need from this planet, while giving nothing in return. He will do all in his power to find solutions to help the planet upon which we live; and, when he does, he will devote his time, energy, and resources to this noble cause with all the loyalty with which he is capable.

The enlightened person with Earth in Aquarius is a child of this Age of Aquarius with noble visions of humanitarianism and clarity of thought. He is forward thinking and fearless in embracing the new ideas and changing consciousness of this

New Age.

Earth in Pisces/Sun in Virgo

People born with The Earth in Pisces have the Sun in the opposite sign of Virgo. Earth in Pisces is a feminine, mutable sign of the Water element, and Virgo is a feminine, mutable sign of the element of Earth. This makes for a very changeable nature. Once they reach up to the magic of their Earth in Pisces, they can overcome a propensity to be fixed in their opinions, as Sun in Virgo tends to be. They can then embrace the wonder of the Cosmos, realizing that nothing is fixed, but everything is flowing—Godwards. They are no longer in control as they previously thought, but God is the ultimate controller; and their job is to allow God, or their Higher Selves, to take control of their lives.

Earth in Pisces is sensitive, fluid, and impractical; but the opposite Sun in Virgo is practical and rather dry, filled with anxieties and obsessed with details. In order for this combination to find their center, there is a strong need to join their need to be practical with something more magical. One way to do this is to strengthen their connection with Mother Earth and Nature, and work in ways that will nurture and care for this beautiful planet.

Earth in Pisces feels centered when they immerse themselves in gardening or yard work. This brings them relief from the dry efficiency that their Sun in Virgo can bring. Virgo is a person who loves rules because it requires them not to have to think too much. However, the magic of life can only be embraced when they reach up to a higher place where there are no rules, only solutions, and this is the place of the magical, mysterious Earth in Pisces. Finding solutions doesn't mean dreaming of what might be, but this means there is work to be done. With this combination, work, effort, and application are their keys for success in achieving their dreams.

The awakened Earth in Pisces has a deep need to make conscious their spiritual nature, imbuing all aspects of their life with a spiritual approach. This innate spirituality is not something for them to bring out on a Sunday or when they are feeling good about life, but at all times and in all ways. This will bring the much-needed motivation to the Sun-in-Virgo side of their nature. This will imbue their work and actions with spiritual desire; and when this happens, this person will then realize that he is here to give service. This is his highest and most noble achievement.

This is sometimes a long path, often achieved later in life. Why? Because the combination of Earth in Pisces and Sun in Virgo is grounded and practical, but these individuals also have a love of ease that holds them back. This can stop them from spending the time and effort in transforming their lower nature into the higher self. Once they overcome this lazy streak by realizing how precious time is, that we are not here to waste it dreaming of what might be, or gazing up at the clouds, or by getting easily distracted, then this combination can achieve very much by setting routines. It is important for the enlightened Earth in Pisces to make time and space within those routines for meditation and reflection on the magic and mystery of life, but not to allow these things to pull them from their center. With this combination, the dreams of Earth in Pisces for a better world are meant to inspire them to action—not fantasy and inaction.

The enlightened Earth in Pisces is not here primarily to achieve their personal goals, but instead to offer their time and energy in service to others despite the personal cost. Then, they can make great progress. When they put all their energy into acquiring position, possessions, or wealth, they will never feel complete. It is only when they rid themselves of all desire, except to be of service, that they can do their best work.

There is a tendency with this combination to harbor fantasies and illusions, refusing to look at things as they really are, but instead, as they would like them to be. Once they overcome this fear (for that is what it is) and if they are courageous enough see things for what they are), then they can be helpful to not only those around them, but to the world as a whole.

As with all the combinations, the path to greater awareness is often slow to achieve and, more than most, this combination can be easily overwhelmed by the realities of life. It is important for these individuals to realize that they may not have the ultimate answers to life that they thought they did. They are rather opinionated and also can easily be led astray by the world of imagination they like to inhabit. They are here learning to be content to carry on in small and quiet ways. In the words of Mother Theresa, *"Never worry about numbers; help one person at a time."*

One of the challenges for the individuals with Earth in Pisces/Sun in Virgo is self-honesty and being able to accept themselves and others, faults and all. They may appear to be cool and calm, while others around them panic, but inside there is often inner anxiety that drives them to strive for perfection in everything they do. Because of this, they are hard on themselves and can end up with frayed nerves and burnout more quickly than some of the more laid-back or carefree signs.

If this happens, they may then spend hours or days of precious time doing nothing much at all. Soon, the busy Sun in the Virgo side of their nature begins to feel uneasy about this, realizing that time is precious and causing them anxiety and fear.

So, how can this person operate efficiently as the Sun in Virgo and delve into the opposite Earth in Pisces to become the best they can possibly be? It's all about learning how to discriminate—a big lifelong lesson for this combination. Knowing when enough is enough, knowing when to relax and enjoy life, and when to work. This usually takes practice, false starts, and wild dreams that lead them astray before they get it right. The good thing with this person is that he is adaptable with a great deal of practicality and common sense, and he can change in the light of greater reason.

Earth in Pisces may sometimes feel bored or disillusioned about having to deal with all the endless minutiae of life. It seems that as much as these individuals manage to organize everything, there is always more to be done. Because of this, they sometimes feel overwhelmed by the sheer volume of details, and this can lead to worry and a feeling that they are not achieving enough. Alternatively, it may cause them to become bored with themselves or with life in general. If this is the case, they should recognize this and see this as a prompting from their higher selves to change.

If you have the Earth in Pisces and Sun in Virgo and boredom hits you, or you experience a feeling of flatness or dullness, realize that now is the time to ground yourself in the non-physical world of music, art, or spirituality, and refuse to be so hard on yourself. Then you can leave the dull, rule-bound life behind to become the discerning, efficient, and helpful person you are meant to be.

They are good at many things from cooking to writing, from painting to plumbing. Not only are they *Jacks of all Trades*, but they are good people, pleasant and easy-going. While they don't like to be taken advantage of and will run a mile if you try, if you genuinely need help, they will be first in line to give you a hand. You will find more doctors, nurses, and healers among this combination than any other; and when you're sick, you'll welcome their gentle, healing touch.

On the other hand, Earth in Pisces/Sun in Virgo is extremely sensitive with regard to his own health. While a physically tougher soul may ignore a headache and pop an aspirin, this person will probably take to his bed and sleep it off. He is attuned to his body more than most, and he realizes that what he needs is not a drug, but rest. Some may think him a hypochondriac, but he just understands the relationship between mind-body and spirit more than most. He knows that when his head aches, it is for a reason. He knows it is his body's way of telling him that he has taken on too much, and it is then that he needs to reach for the power of his Earth in Pisces and withdraw for a while.

For this person, when life becomes too routine and dry, he also needs to laugh and express his innate sense of the hilarious. On the topic of "dry," this person becomes alive around water because he literally can become dry. He should be conscious of drinking enough clean water and take regular dips in the ocean, a nearby lake, or swimming pool. This will help him to relax.

To really live up to the power of Earth in Pisces, the enlightened person must learn and understand what it means to sacrifice himself for a cause bigger than he is. Instead of dividing his life into segments—work time, playtime, household chore time and family time, and sticking rigidly to this self-imposed program, he will really make progress when he is prepared to give up rigid, compulsory routines for something higher and nobler than he is. Then the rigid routines that seem to dry the joy out of life can be replaced by a life in which they express and follow a higher flow.

The awakened Earth in Pisces knows there is more to life than work and routine. He is concerned about global warming and the environment, and he recycles his waste. He has a green thumb and a little garden with organic vegetables. When the global economy collapses, he will be ready. He may not be religious in the accepted sense, but he's the first to lend a helping hand to someone in need. He may not shed a tear when he sees a car accident or the victims of a flood, but he'll be the first to rush in and administer aid.

His kindness and compassion are not showy things, but they are an innate part of who he is. If he can overcome his criticism and his desire for control and order, he can then be prepared to change in the light of greater reason than his own.

Here is a person for whom the Mother Earth can literally be his role model. This beautiful Goddess sacrifices herself for all the millions and millions of tiny life forms upon Her body without any thought of herself. The true power of the enlightened Earth in Pisces will come when greater sacrifice is made: when he moves away from a desire to control and a fixation with the demands of the physical world—including his own health and security—to the demands of the spiritual world. It is then that the enlightened Earth in Pisces will be a spiritual lighthouse in these dark days.

Chapter 7

The Twelve Houses and Their Meaning

"Astrology is a Language. If you understand this language, The Sky Speaks to You."
—Dane Rudhyar

The Horoscope

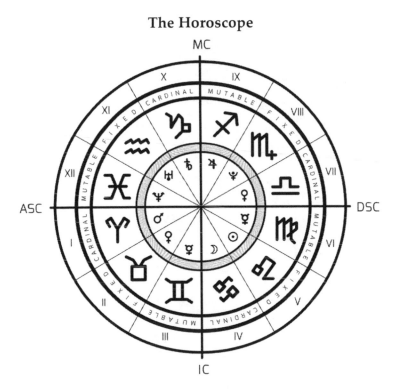

As well as understanding more about the Earth in the different signs of the zodiac, as well as the Sun and all the other planets, it's also important to understand where the planets and signs are located in your own personal horoscope.

Your horoscope, which is based on the date, time and location of your birth, is divided into twelve segments. These segments contain the planets and other astronomical points and are known as "the Houses." The twelve houses are drawn anticlockwise around the chart wheel. The 1st house starts on the east at the nine o'clock position, and this point is known as *the Ascendant* or *Rising Sign*. The 2nd house is at the eight o'clock position and so on, until the 12th house, the final segment.

When you look at the diagram above, you will see that each house is numbered I through XII, and each house is significant because it is like a different room or scene in your personal play. These houses represent your relationships, your career, your home, your family, your aspirations, your health, and so on. Another way to think of the houses is as twelve different rooms of a mansion. There are certain places in your twelve-room mansion that you would naturally end up spending more time in than you would the others, and so it is that way with your horoscope.

The Twelve Houses of the Horoscope

There is a quick way to understand the *meanings* of the twelve houses. Their themes are similar to the twelve zodiac signs, which are the natural rulers of the houses. The first sign, Aries, influences the activity of the 1st house; the second sign, Taurus, influences the 2nd house; and so on round your horoscope. Become familiar with the signs of the zodiac, and then the themes of each house will become clearer. As with any shortcut, it is not perfect, but it will get you going in the right direction.

Each house has a *natural* ruler and also an *actual ruler*. The natural ruler always rules the house and never changes. For example, the natural ruler of the 1st house is always Aries, and the natural ruler of the 4th house is always Cancer, the fourth sign of the zodiac. The *actual ruler* of your house changes according to when and where you were born, so it is specific to you.

The 1st House – I am

This describes your personality, physical appearance, whether your hair is long, black, or short, or green. It's how tall you are and whether you're likely to put on weight. It's how others see you. The natural ruler of this house is Aries. This house is all about you and it is the opposite House to the 7th, which is about your relationships. If you were born with the sign of Leo on your 1st house cusp (the Ascendant), you radiate the pride and confidence of Leo, with vitality and personal magnetism.

The 2nd house – I possess

This house describes your sense of self-worth, your value system, and it explains how you earn *and spend* money. The natural ruler is Taurus. It gives an idea of what's important to you and whether you still have your cuddly toys from childhood. It is your values, as opposed to the values of another, indicated by the opposite house, the 8th. If you have Capricorn ruling your 2nd house, you are cautious and conservative with your finances, and you understand the value of things and how to make money.

The 3rd house – I communicate

This house describes how your mind works. This is your everyday analytical mind, as opposed to your intuitive mind, indicated by the opposite House—the 9th. The natural ruler is Gemini. This is where you learn your times tables and work out your shopping lists. It is your primary education. It's also a place of movement and shows if you're light on your feet. It indicates short trips and also relationships to siblings and neighbors. If you have Aquarius ruling your 3rd house, you like to think outside the box and have a broad, objective and independent mind.

The 4th house – I feel

This is the house of home and it shows if you prefer a rambling country estate or a flat or loft in the city. It is your roots and your inner self. The natural ruler is Cancer. Its opposite house is the 10th and that is about you in the world, your career and vocation; the 4th is about you at home. It's also about how you feel and whether you dredge up memories from the past or keep them hidden. It rules your parent, usually your mother, as well as your family history and country. If you have Taurus ruling your 4th house, you like your home to be comfortable and traditional, with quality furniture and artwork.

The 5th house – I create

This is the recreational house. It is your creative expression, romance and love affairs, gambling and speculation, fun and games. The natural ruler is Leo. You can see from a person's 5th House whether he is a budding Picasso and how likely he is to have children. The house also describes your children or your inner child. It's about giving love while its opposite House, the 11th describes how you receive love. If you have Sagittarius ruling your 5th house, you enjoy sports, such as horse riding and archery and enjoy learning and foreign travel.

The 6th house – I analyze

This indicates the state of your physical health and your interest in this. Are you a pill-popper or do you prefer the natural way? It also describes your daily routines and interaction with co-workers if you have them. The natural ruler is Virgo. It tells of your attention to detail and striving for perfection. Its opposite House, the 12th, is about submerging the details in your quest for Oneness. If you have Cancer ruling your 6th house, your health reflects your sensitive emotions. You do well in a home-based business, or you like your work place to be a second home.

The 7th house – I relate

This is all about your partnerships (marriage or business). The natural ruler is Libra. It shows whether you are likely to marry and, if so, whether you would prefer a husband like your father or one more like your son. It's how you commit and also what you are prepared to give in a relationship. The 7th is your appreciation for the arts, your love of fair play and harmony. If you have Scorpio ruling your 7th house (also known as *the Descendant*), your relationships are intense, controlling, and secretive. You prize emotional closeness and sharing.

The 8th house – I desire

This is your mysterious place of sex, death, sharing, rebirth, your psychic nature, and transformation. If you can't see the connection, it is probably because it is mysterious like its natural ruler, Scorpio. If you are married, this house indicates whether your spouse has the funds of Oprah or whether you need to support her. It's her worth, as opposed to your own. On a mystic level, this house indicates your transformation as you make the ultimate surrender not to another person, but to God. If you have Libra ruling your 8th house, you want your sharing and intimate relationships to be fair and just, and on equal terms.

The 9th house – I teach

This house shows whether you are likely to be a high-school dropout or a college professor. It is the state of your higher education and also your higher, intuitive mind. You may be a high-school dropout but have the inspiration and intuition of a visionary. The natural ruler is Sagittarius. It is the opposite house to the 3rd house, your everyday mind. This House rules publishing, your philosophy of life, and religious beliefs. Whereas the 3rd House is short-distance travel, the 9th House is foreign places and overseas travel. It shows your attitude to the future and to the unknown. If you have Pisces ruling your 9th house, you will dream of faraway places. You are intuitive, but you could be an absent-minded professor.

The 10th house – I plan

The 10th house is opposite the 4th house of home and represents your public self and career. With a strong 10th house, you can be born penniless in a Third World country and end up ruling the world. The natural ruler is Capricorn and it shows your willpower, how you make your way in the world, and how you are perceived in society. It indicates your ambitions and how you can reach them. It describes your father, mother, or an authority figure in your family. If you have Gemini ruling your 10th house, your career involves your mind and dexterity, and you would make a good teacher, writer, or dancer.

The 11th house – I inspire

This house describes your friends and whether or not they are dull and reliable or extraordinary and brilliant. It shows what kind of friend you are and also your humanitarianism. It's how likely you are to join a political party and camp outside in the snow for the sake of human rights. It shows if you are motivated to join together with people of like minds in groups for the common good. The natural ruler is Aquarius. It is your idealism and vision for the future. It rules sudden events, rebellion, and outrageousness. If you have Virgo ruling your 11th house, you are discriminating in your friendships and group associations, as well as loyal and helpful.

The 12th house – I heal

This is the last house in your horoscope, and it is your house of self-undoing, as well as spirituality and healing. It's not an easy place to experience because what you are *really doing* is undoing all the ties that bind you to material life in your search for spirituality and enlightenment. It's also your karma, good and bad. Its natural ruler is Pisces. It is your subconscious and where you can deceive yourself. It also indicates hospitals and institutions, serving others through compassion, psychic ability, and sensitivity. If you have Aries ruling your 12th house, your sense of self is connected with your spirituality. You are prepared to sacrifice yourself for God or a cause greater than you.

You have read above about the natural rulers of each house. As mentioned, these themes of the houses are now overlaid by the signs of the zodiac on the cusp of each house of your horoscope when you were born. Look at your horoscope and see the signs dotted around the edge of the chart wheel. These signs add flavor to the activity of each house. If you have glamorous Leo on your 4th house of home, you like a ritzy, expensive home with frequent dinner parties and social activity. If you have mercurial Gemini on the cusp of your 7th house, communication is important in your relationships. Stability and reliability would not necessarily be what you are seeking (depending upon other factors in your horoscope), but discussion and sharing ideas would be essential.

Chapter 8

The Earth through the Houses

"The soul of the newly born baby is marked for life by the pattern of the stars at the moment it comes into the world, unconsciously remembers it, and remains sensitive to the return of configurations of a similar kind."
—Johannes Kepler, Harmonies of the World

Chapter 6 explains what you can expect if you have Earth in Aries or Earth in Gemini in your horoscope. Because the horoscope moves according to the time and place you were born, you could have your Earth in Aries, for example, in the 1st House, or it could be in the 7th or any other House. This adds another "flavor" or dimension to your Earth in Aries. For example, if it is in the 1st House (the natural ruler of which is Aries), it is a double-whammy and would greatly strengthen the effect of your Earth in Aries. If it falls in the 10th House, you may put your talents to use in your career.

The Influence of Earth in the Twelve Houses

Earth in the 1st House

With the Earth in the 1st House, you have the Sun in the opposite 7th House which is about the "Other", i.e., relationships of all types. It is through these personal relationships that you face challenges, overcome struggles, as well as learn compromise and love. Once you do this, you can truly become an individual. Your soul's expression on this physical realm is about using your awakened self for a higher, nobler cause. This may require working in partnership or in teams with others of like mind, but you are in a good position to lead the team. You have a particular affinity for Mother Earth and, once awakened to the power of the Earth in your chart, you are seen by others as a powerful Ambassador—intelligent and focused regarding your cause. In your quest for the perfect relationship as expressed by your Sun in the 7th House, you will find the ultimate relationship in your connection to Mother Earth. This can bring you not only harmony and solace, but also self-healing.

Earth in the 2nd House

You are an intense personality with your Sun in the 8th House, digging deep below surface appearances to find truth. You are the person who may suffer a serious setback or extreme challenge and, after an intense struggle, bounce back totally renewed and ready to fight another day. When you fully awaken to the power of your Earth in the 2nd House, you will find this a wonderful position. Instead of using your significant power to control others or become obsessed about some object of your desire, you are now able to use it as a reservoir of life energy, vitality, and spiritual resources. It's important for you to go out into Nature—to touch the flowers and the trees, to feel the breeze on your face. You will value your connection to the Earth as never before. This physical connection to Mother Earth will bring you balance and give you the ability to go through difficult, intense and challenging circumstances, and then transform yourself. Now you will realize that your true power is not the power you have over others, but the inner power that you can use to inspire and uplift others.

Earth in the 3rd House

You are the student of life, the adventurer and the traveler, with your Sun in the 9th House. But, when you fully awaken to your Earth in the 3rd House, you are ready to also be the teacher. In astrology, the 9th House represents the higher mind where true intuition is born; the 3rd House is the conscious mind of intelligence and discernment. When your intuition and intelligence are united, you are ready to understand and express your soul's destiny on this physical realm. You are no longer always dreaming of change and the next adventure, never quite sure where these will lead you. By becoming more conscious of the influence of Earth in the 3rd House, this adds a practical element. You can now discern whether your dreams are just idle ideas or whether they can make a positive contribution to life. You are now ready to express your ideals and adventurous spirit. Combined with your powers of discernment and your intelligence, you are ready to communicate and teach the truth about the important things in life.

Earth in the 4th House

With the Earth in the 4th House and the Sun in the opposite 10th House, you are a person who may be driven by ambition and can be very successful in the public eye or in a career. You are born to be out there in the world making a difference. However, until you are more aware of your Earth in the 4th House, you may feel there is something missing from the very foundation of your life. You may then retreat or reject this desire for achievement in the world. When you consciously draw upon your Earth energy you find the balance you seek, and this will stabilize you. You can use this power to stoke up your inner fires, and you may decide to build a "meditation zone" or home office and decorate it with "fruits of the Earth," such as a fountain and plants to help you attune to this loving energy of Mother Earth. Temper your ambitions with your innate love of Mother Earth and your own nurturing instincts, for these are vital for your happiness and success. Express your gratitude and appreciation for the Earth, and this will bring you the harmony and balance you need in your busy life.

Earth in the 5th House

You are a person with high ideals who wants to change society and transform the world for you have the Sun in the 11th House of ideals and aspirations. When you see injustice, you are stirred to action, and you want to make a difference; but it is when you consciously draw on the power of your Earth in the opposite 5th House that you stimulate your true inner power. In fact, it is when you do this that you will more fully inhabit your courage, creativity, and willpower, and it is then that you can really make a difference. It is these innate qualities and attributes that will drive you and enable you to not just be an idealist but to live your ideals and use your power to help and transform your life in a positive way. At a higher level, with Earth in the 5th House, your sense of soul's purpose will be focused towards the children of the world and the future of life on Mother Earth.

Earth in the 6th House

Your power lies in the fact that with your Sun in the opposite 12th House, you are a soul-centered individual. You may not truly feel at home on this physical plane of Earth until you consciously draw on the power of having Earth in the 6th House, which represents your daily work. You innately feel a sense of the magical and the spiritual but, until you ground these feelings through your work, express them through your everyday life, and follow your heart by helping and healing those less fortunate, you can become lost or lonely. The power of your Earth is vitally important for your self-healing and happiness; it motivates you and helps you to bring your dreams to reality. It allows you to make your faith a living thing. Activate this power by walking in nature and opening yourself up to the beauty and magic of the realms of nature spirits and devas. This will feed you spiritually and strengthen you through the challenges of life. The Earth in the 6th House can potentially be the most spiritual of all once you have learned how to use this wonderful energy through the healing and service you give.

Earth in the 7th House

You have the Sun in your 1st House and this places the emphasis on you, the individual. You are strong, active, vital, and magnetic physically, with a personality that is noticed! You are a natural leader with intelligence and many fine qualities, but it is when you draw on the power of your Earth in the 7th House that the true magic begins. Relationships, partnership, and teamwork are keys for you, while always remaining true to yourself and your own unique contribution to life. In order to keep this balance of yourself and another person, it's essential for you to have downtime or retreat into nature on a regular basis. Here, you will find yourself; here you will strengthen your inner self, restore harmony, and re-connect with the one relationship that will always nurture you—Mother Earth. You are a person who is confident, one who has a strong, positive ego and, when you find a noble cause that inspires you, you are able to sacrifice yourself for something that you recognize is greater than you are.

Earth in the 8th House

You are a person who enjoys a pleasant, comfortable lifestyle, and you love nature and the beautiful things of life. You have a strong sense of you own self-worth. While others struggle, you seem to be able to draw bounty into your life. However, there is a part of you calling you to change and transform—that is the call of the Earth in the 8th House. When your life is too steady, then the Earth calls you to further develop your talents and resources for the good of others. If you refuse to listen, your life becomes drier as your vital energy decreases. When you follow these inner promptings, you may be led towards challenges and trials but these represent the battleground in which your personal transformation can take place. When you avoid this higher calling, your true power and potential will slip away. When you are prepared to move forward bravely and give more despite the cost, then the Earth will provide you with the strength you need. As a result, you will grow and gain the spiritual power that you seek.

Earth in the 9th House

You are a communicator, a messenger, and a teacher with the Sun in your 3rd House. You love knowledge and you are mentally bright and active with a thousand ideas. You enjoy collecting information, and you love the diversity of different beliefs and thought systems. You love to learn and are an eternal student and will probably enjoy higher education. However, because of this tendency of being interested in everything, you can be scattered and lose sight of your main goals and ambitions in life. When you consciously draw on the power of your Earth in the 9th House, you will find unity amidst the diversity. You can draw on this source of power by allowing yourself quiet times in which you listen to the voice of your intuition as it speaks to you. This combination, as well as being intelligent, is also potentially highly intuitive. Then, when this part of you speaks, you will find you are no longer scattered in different directions but you are ready to focus on your higher calling. This will bring you better health, more vitality, and a strong sense of purpose, which will energize your life with Love.

Earth in the 10th House

You have a rich inner life and strong foundations with your Sun in the 4th House of home and inner self. You like quiet, peaceful times and you enjoy your home and family. You are a person who may consider working from home, or you may enjoy renovating or working on your home. You also need retreats away from the hustle and bustle of life. However, the energy of your Earth in the 10th House is calling you to leave the comfort of your home and venture out into the world, to stoke up the fires of your ambitions. When you ignore this call, you can become too wrapped up in challenges of the home and family, with little time for your own goals. It is important for you to become more conscious and awakened to this silent prompting of the Mother Earth, which is your true home, and it is urging you to become more visible in the world. You may express your nurturing nature through a career and public role, or you can also use this considerable power to effect positive social change. It is then that you will feel truly fulfilled.

Earth in the 11th House

With the Sun in the opposite 5th House, you are creative and courageous, with a strong will and natural leadership abilities. You enjoy life with the creativity you feel, and you enjoy spending time with children. The hallmark of the Aquarian Age in which we are now living, is group activities. When we get together with other people of like-mind in service for the common good, we can achieve far more than we can on our own. You have the Earth in the 11th House and it is calling you to do just that, to use your tremendous creativity and *joie de vivre* for the common good. You are a person who has already developed a healthy ego over the lifetimes; now the Earth is calling you to work with others in groups to achieve your spiritual goals, and your collective purpose of humanity's evolutionary development. The power of the Earth is teaching you that you are a child of this Aquarian Age and, as such, you may be drawn to the new sciences, including astrology, and use these to benefit humanity and the Earth in some way.

Earth in the 12th House

With the Sun in the opposite 6th House, you are organized, efficient, and geared to the challenges of everyday life. You are also kindhearted and ready to lend a helping hand. However, until you consciously draw the power of Earth into your life, you may find yourself on an endless cycle of routine, which can be stressful and affect your health. Healing can take place when you contact the wonderful source of beauty and power available to you through the placement of Earth in your 12th House. This is the House of spirituality and sacrifice of your own desires and routines for something bigger and more important than you are. This may take the form of a deep Earth-based spirituality or a strong desire to give service to those less fortunate. Whenever you follow these promptings, you will know that you are on the right track and these promptings and desires will ground you, de-stress, and heal you. In our evolutionary journey, we are all learning to align our personal will with the Will of the soul, or God. It is especially essential for you to do this to achieve true inner joy and sense of fulfillment.

SECTION III

RECONNECTING TO THE EARTH'S ENERGY

Chapter 9

How to Connect with Mother Earth

"Walk as if you are kissing the Earth with your feet."
—Thích Nhất Hạnh

This Chapter examines how we can attune more closely to the planet Earth in our horoscopes and in our lives, as did ancient civilizations—but in a way that is in keeping with this New Age. There are personal exercises, meditations, visualizations, and grounding techniques to improve our physical, mental, and spiritual health. More importantly, this Chapter explains how we can not only learn how to attune to the Earth, but how we can gain a right relationship with this planet as a living entity. The Earth and our relationship to Her is not only the missing jigsaw piece in astrology, but this is also the missing piece in the jigsaw that is the evolution of humanity.

Ways to Reconnect

In order for us to reconnect with Mother Earth, first we must become more conscious and aware of the importance of this attunement, and to be grateful and appreciative for this beautiful planet upon which we all live.

It is said that where the mind goes, energy follows. When we are conscious and appreciative of Mother Earth, we are sending energy of our love and gratitude to Her. By the law of karma, what we send out comes back to us, thus setting up a deeper relationship with our divine Mother. We are then anchoring ourselves in the correct way; we are re-establishing the correct, long lost foundation for our lives; and this in turn will bring to us a spiritual sense of calm, peace, love, and Oneness with the Earth.

Whenever we can attune to this deep feeling of peace, it has beneficial effects on our health. Since most disease begins in the aura—the subtle bodies that surround our physical body—it is essential for us to not only strive for good physical health, but also to maintain strong, healthy auras. One powerful way we can do this is through the Violet Flame Practice.

The Violet Flame Practice

The Violet Flame comes from the beloved Mother Earth whenever we request this most sacred and protective mystic practice. This practice, used by the Spiritual Hierarchy of Earth, has only been available in the ancient mystery schools and has been a closely guarded secret for thousands of years.

Now, in this new Aquarian Age when the waters of truth are being offered freely to humanity, this was first introduced to the world by The Master Aetherius. This great Cosmic Master channeled this sacred practice through Dr. George King so that everyone could have access to—and more importantly—use this practice.[7]

How to Use the Violet Flame Practice

Very simply, we visualize this Violet Flame coming up through us from Mother Earth beneath our feet. Imagine or visualize this beautiful soft Violet Flame, cleansing and transmuting the lower energies in our aura, purifying and strengthening us. Doing this practice is particularly essential in these days of increased microwaves and electromagnetic fields (EMF). If we do this practice often enough and with as much love, focus, and concentration as we can, this practice can strengthen our auras and protect us against these artificial waves.

One of the very best ways to practice the Violet Flame, and so reconnect with Mother Earth, is to go barefoot in nature when you can, and if the weather permits, and physically stand on the Earth. In this way, you can really feel the wonderful, loving, cleansing Violet Flame coming from the living heart of the Earth

Herself.

Breathe deeply and rhythmically until you feel calm and relaxed.

Then, visualize a violet-colored flame coming up from the ground beneath your feet. Try to feel this as a velvety flame, not hot, but a cool, velvet flame caressing your body and aura.

Then, once you have visualized this, draw the Violet Flame right up through your body and aura to about 20, 30 feet or more above your head. Do not limit this visualization.

You will see that this is a very simple practice but do not be fooled by its simplicity. This is a flame of great power from the very heart of the Mother Earth; and when you invoke it through your imagination, this will flow through you in a mighty force of cleansing and protection, so essential in these days.

The Realms of Nature

"If we can communicate with nature, it is because it is alive and intelligent. And it is alive and intelligent because it is inhabited by creatures that are probably invisible to us but are nevertheless very real. These creatures, which we call gnomes, undines, sylphs and salamanders, have been mentioned in the various traditions around the world but by other names."
—Omraam Mikhael Aivanhov

The Earth is a beautiful planet, as we know, and her bountiful nature is able to feed us and give us all we need to survive. As well as this, Earth also has upon her body, living realms of nature. All of us can begin to see, feel, be aware of and attune more fully to these invisible, but tangible realms.

Astrology is one metaphysical discipline that teaches the five elements. From this study, we learn that we are composed of and interact with these elements—Fire, Earth, Air, Water—and the fifth element—Ether—every moment, and so it is important to have an understanding of these elements. The Element of the twelve signs of the zodiac, for example, shows a specific type of consciousness.

The elements are the gears of life, which must mesh in harmony for there to be health of mind and body. They are like plates in a battery through which life energy (prana) flows to energize them. Every different sign of the zodiac relates to a different element—Aries is the Fire element, Capricorn the Earth element, Pisces the Water element, Aquarius the Air element, and so on.

On the subtle realms of Earth, there are a variety of non-physical beings—known as the *devic kingdom*, or the realms of nature—that work with the elements. It is said that in the days of Atlantis we walked and communed with these beings. Now, since we have on the whole lost our connection with Mother Earth, we have no knowledge of them. However, despite our acknowledgement of them, they continue to use our energy, good, bad, and indifferent, to create conditions on the surface of Earth.

They can only produce the weather and conditions on this planet according to the energy we give them. When we give them hate, they can only create chaotic conditions; and when we give love, they can then create the harmony that is our destiny.

Humanity has a direct link with these elementals because we are composed not only of flesh, blood, and bones and an array of chemicals but also of these five elements (Fire, Earth, Air, Water, and Ether).

Through my own life's experiences, I have learned that these elementals, also known as nature spirits or devas, are very responsive and ready for conscious interaction with humans. They want us to be aware of them and work with them. Indigenous cultures also will remind us of this and perform sacred ceremonies to attune and work with these intelligences to gain a right relationship with them and Mother Earth.

Wherever we go, it's good to become aware of the presence of all these entities which already existed a long time before we humans appeared. Make friends with them, speak to them, be amazed at the work they carry out both underground and above ground, in water, in air, in fire, and in the earth. Quite often, they will be so happy that they will bring you gifts of energy, joy, poetic inspiration, and even clairvoyance.

Recently, when I was recovering from some serious surgery, I was sitting on the patio and my husband took a photo. What appeared in the photo, apart from me, was a little deva! They are around us all the time!

One of the preeminent people who studied, communed with, and wrote about his experiences with the devic kingdom, was the Theosophist, Geoffrey Hodson. He wrote several books about this invisible, but very real realm of nature. His fascinating book, *The Kingdom of the Gods* contains information about many of the devas—from the vast mountain devas to devas present at religious ceremonies and spiritual events. He was able to not only clairvoyantly see the devas but also to commune with them. To him, the devas were just as real as people—if not more so—and he described their rituals and their roles in his wonderful books.

My Spiritual Master, Dr. George King, was not only aware of the devic kingdom, but he taught about this and was able to commune with them. More importantly, he devised global healing missions, one of which sends very high frequency energy to the devic kingdom, which in turn helps to bring about a stabilization of natural conditions upon Earth.

Everyday Connections with the Devas

There are also simple things we can do to commune with the devas every day of our lives.

We can go out into nature and be conscious and aware of the work of the devas and nature spirits. When we see a beautiful flower, be aware of the little nature spirit who tends to this blossom. When we see a majestic tree, perhaps hundreds of years old, try and tune into to the equally majestic deva of that tree: strong, real, alive, just as we are. But let us not just tune into them, let us also offer them our appreciation through a prayer or a few words of gratitude for their ceaseless and vitally important work on our beautiful green planet.

Let us go out into nature alone if we can, or with someone of like mind. As we offer our gratitude, spend a few minutes quietly awaiting the devas' response. You will feel it, and some of you may even see the devas. There have been times when I have smelled a beautiful perfume after offering appreciation to the devas. I have seen them twice in my life—but always, and most definitely, I feel a beautiful uplifting response.

A few times recently, Gary and I have gone to Northern Michigan, and there are places there that are virtually untouched by humans. We walked into one such place, and immediately we both felt a strong resistance from the devas of this place. We definitely felt unwelcome as if we had disturbed them, as indeed we had. We immediately sent out our love to them and both offered our prayers of gratitude, and immediately the atmosphere changed. It was so remarkable and so sudden a change that we both stopped in our tracks.

This was a beautiful example to us both of how quickly the devas and nature spirits respond to our energy. It brought home to us both just how responsible we are for the energy that we constantly radiate, realizing as we do that this is the energy that the devas use to create world conditions. We can never blame the weather for a flood or drought, for although created by the devas, it is humanity that provides the energy—love and hate, and everything in between.

Deva Houses

There are devas in nature, but there are also devas of place; and no doubt you have devas in your home who were probably there before you were. Gary and I like to attune and honor the devas in our home by providing a little wooden "deva house" which is set up in the corner of our living room. We leave symbolic food and water in front of the house as a demonstration of our appreciation and caring for these little devas.

While we have not actually seen these devas, we both feel them. If we go away on a vacation or a trip, we let the devas know what we are doing and when we expect to return. We ask them to protect our home and offer them a prayer of gratitude. It's when we return that we feel their presence intensely! Both of us are aware of them jumping and leaping around, as if they are so glad we are home. We do not have the lifestyle to have cats or dogs, but we take care of the wildlife in our garden—the birds, squirrels, chipmunks—and we also take care of our beautiful little devas!

Like anything else, becoming more conscious of the devas and nature spirits, takes vigilance and practice. However, it is a wonderful thing to do, and this practice will bring you much joy and love into your life.

In the days of the ancient civilization of Atlantis, we did walk and talk with the devas, but our current disconnect is yet another sign of our dissociation from the Earth. However, we all can begin to re-establish this vitally important connection in a very positive and loving way. By incorporating positive practices in our daily lives, we shall be helping to improve conditions upon the surface of this planet.

Earth's Ancient Mysteries

We have discussed ways in which we can reconnect with our sacred Mother Earth—directly through offering our appreciation and gratitude, through the Violet Flame practice and indirectly through working with Her kingdom of nature—the Devic Kingdom. And yet, what can we do to help the Earth Herself?

First of all, we must understand a little of Her ancient mysteries and Her Spiritual nature.

Poets, writers, and mystics have always known that nature contains within it some intangible mystery that certain places on the Earth's surface are more inspiring and uplifting than others. Often, these same places coincide with centers of prehistoric importance and sanctity, and previous civilizations attuned to the planet through a deeper understanding of this sacred geometry and energy patterns.

Aerial photographs have been taken over parts of the world, especially Britain, renowned for ancient mysteries; and the first impression is the vast number of regular geometric lines that crisscross the country. Many researchers believe these were set in prehistoric times. This is like a geometry-based grid system.

The true and full purpose of this terrestrial geometry is still unclear but points to previous civilizations that took into account the natural elements and energies, as well as the position of the Sun, Moon, and planets, and used a form of spiritual engineering, which is difficult to comprehend fully today.

One thing that becomes clear is that there is definitely a connection between this grid system, known as *ley lines*, and links to sacred sites, UFOs, astrology, and consciousness. There is an incredible connectedness that is revealed. Ancient civilizations knew, as did indigenous cultures, and we are discovering again today that we are part of something larger—there is a divine order. We, together with the Earth, the Sun, and the Galaxy are all living beings evolving back to God.

It became clear that ley lines weren't just tracks and footpaths. Many researchers found that the ley system *as well as* being tracks also marked a flow of current from the Earth—a natural flow of force related to Earth's magnetic field. Researchers also found that sacred sites, churches, standing stones, etc., were at significant points. Interestingly, animals followed these tracks instinctively.

The accuracy of the lines and the way they selected sacred spots shows their construction was performed by people with a deep understanding of the hidden nature of the countryside.

A German geographer, Dr. Heinrich, spoke of some lost magical principles by which the sites of holy centers had been located in the remote past. His research indicated some sites were placed on lines of great geometrical figures, which were related to the position of the heavenly bodies. He believed this was evidence of a universal civilization with advanced knowledge of science and magic. Another researcher, Foster Forbes, found sacred sites laid out to reflect the constellations.

Even today, the names of hills and mounds often coincide with an aspect of the sun, moon, a star, or with the spiritual principle it represents. Many believe that the whole landscape of Britain has been laid out to a celestial pattern.

It is interesting that Dr. King said that the British Isles are very significant, not the people—but the actual land. There are important ley lines, sacred places, a sacred entrance to the Earth, chakras of Earth—land based and water based—as well as Holy Mountains.

However, it's not just about the ancient land of Britain—tracks and leys in Britain have exact parallels in South America. There are sacred places all over the world, including the Great Pyramid of Egypt, the standing stones of Carnac, France; the etheric city of Shamballa, known as the jewel or the Crown Chakra of Earth over the Gobi Desert; Mount Shasta, California—a Retreat of the Spiritual Hierarchy of Earth; Stonehenge, England—over 5,000 years old and still one of the great mysteries of Earth—and many more.

The purpose for which stone monuments of the ancient world were so carefully sited can be understood through the ideals of the builders—these were very different from the ideals of modern science. The builders recognized the Earth as a living being, in a living universe whose health and prosperity was bound up with that of its inhabitants.

The Earth as a Spiritual and Sacred Intelligence

Most importantly, we should always remember that the Earth is not here for us. She is a highly evolved living Intelligence, far above us in Her evolution and advancement. Out of Her great compassion, She provides a home for us in Space and gives us all we need to sustain us. In return, we take everything from Her for the most part, with little or no thought for this great and mighty Goddess.

While ecology is a very good thing for it helps humanity, an even greater and more important type of ecology is that which helps Earth Herself. Perhaps a strange concept for many, but this type of belief has been held by many indigenous cultures throughout history.

The Earth is indeed a conscious, living, breathing Intelligence—just as are all the planets; and this, I believe, is the *raison d'etre* for astrology and why it works. The living planets are constantly radiating their energy like a great cosmic symphony to help all life in its multitudinous forms in their journeys through evolution.

Chapter 10

Our Future on Planet Earth

"The Earth does not belong to us. We belong to the Earth."
—Chief Seattle

The future is up to us. Mother Earth has done all she can to help us, protect us, as we move slowly, life after life, for the most part in a completely selfish frenzy of trying to take as much as we can from this beautiful, fruitful planet.

Astrology can only do so much. It can help to make us more aware of Earth's power, Her influence, Her incredible energies that are helping us to evolve and transform and become worthy of being Her children. However, this growing realization of the part the Earth plays in all our lives must be acted upon if we are to survive. The good news is that there are a million and one ways in which we can help reconnect in powerful and positive ways to Mother Earth. They are expressed through gratitude, appreciation, visualization, ritual, and prayer. We can connect to her through working in selfless ways to protect and preserve Her fruits—nature, the oceans and waterways.

One thing we have to do to keep up with this ever-evolving Intelligence is to become more aware and more enlightened ourselves. We also must change our perspective and realize that even if we reconnect with the Earth through the ways given in this book and in other ways also, we still are missing the main point. While it is good for us—essential for us—absolutely wonderful for us—if we do once again re-establish this ancient connection to our Divine Mother, this does not benefit Her—only us. However, I believe that once we do work hard to re-establish this connection, we shall at the same time grow in our love and appreciation for the Earth. By doing this, we shall come to realize that the most important thing is to do all we can to take care of Mother Earth Herself, our home.

The Earth has sacrificed enough—far too much—for us. While we take everything we want from Her without even so much as a "thank you," let alone asking permission, we rarely ever consider whether this is good for Her. If we believe She is a living Intelligence, (and we know she is), and if we believe that She is far more enlightened than we shall be for millions of years to come, then by the law of logic alone, we must pay far more attention to Her needs.

This is particularly important now when some prominent thinkers believe we are on the brink of destruction of the human race, including even the distinguished scientist, inventor, and author, James Lovelock, who proposed the hopeful Gaia hypothesis: that the biosphere is a self-regulating entity with the capacity to keep our planet healthy.

The Disconnect Today

Scientific American told the story of a young boy in the US who said, *"I like to play indoors better because that's where the electrical outlets are."* This shows how disconnected children are from nature and a study revealed that kids ages eight to eighteen spend an average of seven and a half hours a day, seven days a week plugged into computers, TV, video games, music, and cell phones.[8]

It is the same in the British Isles, and probably all over the world. According to the Department for Environment, Food and Rural Affairs, the likelihood of a child visiting any sizeable outside green space has halved in just one generation. Today, many children, and increasingly adults, suffer from this growing disconnect with Mother Earth and Her fruits—nature.

While this disconnect is definitely not a new phenomenon and the seeds were planted around the time of the Industrial Revolution, the problem has worsened exponentially since the advent of the personal computer. Life is better because of this in many ways but, as far as our health is concerned and the health of our children, these have been impacted in a negative manner.

Also, things are becoming even worse, as studies show that more parents worry today about their children picking up germs and diseases from insects so that schools are cutting back on field trips. However, research shows that children are not only happier and more creative—and also healthier—when they have a connection to nature. Adults heal faster in hospitals when they have a view of nature from their windows.

It is obvious when we think about it but, on the whole, not enough is being done to change things. As a result we are rapidly losing our vitally important connection to Mother Earth.

Interestingly, a renowned biologist, E.O. Wilson, believes that humanity is hard-wired with an innate affinity for Nature and he calls this *"biophilia."* Tragically, research has shown that if children do not have the opportunity to develop this affinity early on, they may actually develop the opposite—an aversion to nature, a fear of being in nature, or even a contempt.

This fear and contempt is then fueled by all the natural disasters about which we hear on a too regular basis. These include earthquakes, volcanic eruptions, and extreme weather conditions. Not for one moment do we stop and think that perhaps this is happening as intensely as it is because we are disconnected to the Earth. Indigenous cultures tell us that we are out of attunement with Her and it is increasingly obvious that we are.

So what can we do? Are we, our children, and our grand-children doomed to physical and mental health problems by the increased technology and lack of interest in the beauty of the natural world all around us?

When we become aware of the seriousness of the problem, it is then that we must begin to act. There are many ways to develop a love and appreciation for nature and to pass this on to our children and grandchildren. One way to develop a sense of awe and wonder is to visit beautiful places. If you are able, schedule a vacation to somewhere as spectacular as the Grand Canyon or the massive sequoia trees in Northern California.

Wherever you live in the world, there are beautiful places that will inspire and uplift you. We are fortunate that we are on such a beautiful, verdant planet; let us be grateful for this.

Indigenous Cultures

The indigenous cultures on the whole, especially those of the Native American lineage, understand the vital importance of our connection with the Earth better than most.

On July 3, 2016 at 4:30 in the morning, I was awoken from a deep sleep by what I believe was a Native American presence. At the time, I was writing my latest book, Mother Earth. The Native American Guide, who I later believed was Chief Tau-Gu of the Paiute Tribe from the Lake Powell, Utah area, and with whom I had been in contact with previously on several occasions, gave me several lines of what seemed like a poem. It was very clear, and the impetus was strong enough that it got me out of bed and onto my computer at this ungodly hour of the morning. The words were a beautiful poem:

"We are spinning, spinning
Out of control
The rain dances cease
and the drought comes
The devas of storm
Bring flood
And we curse.
Cut off from Divine Mother
We are spinning, spinning
Out of control."
—Native American Guide

I love poetry and write it, but these were not my own words. As well as this cryptic but wise message, I also received other advice that made me re-assess the book. It was then in its final stages but I knew it was back to the drawing board.

I first met this guide—or rather he met me *"the Englishwoman"*—when I was in the Lake Powell area. Since then, I have received advice on health and herbs. Additionally, he has also helped with a very powerful bone-healing technique when my husband was giving me healing one day.

My point of telling this story is two-fold. First of all, I may not have met this guide initially, had I not left my computer for a while and gone out into the ancient beauty of the Lake Powell area. Secondly, it was proof that we do have guides and that they are aware of what we are doing. It was clear to me that the Chief was aware of what I was writing because his words did sum up, in only ten lines, the whole hypothesis of my book!

Dr. George King taught that all Spirituality should have at its heart—The Earth. Many of the indigenous cultures understand this, such as the Native American culture here in the USA. We in the so-called civilized world can learn a lot from many of the indigenous cultures worldwide who still regard the Earth as a sacred Being, not a resource from which to take everything they can.

What Can We Do to Help Mother Earth?

First, we can understand and appreciate Her sacrifice for us, Her own advancement and the Primary Initiation she underwent on July 8, 1964, and realize just how fortunate we are to be here. There is a law governing us all and that is the Law of Karma. By this great Law of divine justice, Mother Earth, as an extremely advanced Intelligence, will not be allowed to continue to suffer on our behalf indefinitely. There will come a time when Her true status will shine forth in glory in the heavens; and since Her Primary Initiation, this is gradually beginning to take place. This will be a wonderful time for those who are spiritually ready for this great change. However, there are those who are not, and it will be a time of great global turmoil, and we are already beginning to see this happening upon Earth.

What we can do—and what we must do—because Spiritual action is no longer just a choice we make, but a necessity, if we wish to remain on this Earth in future lives, is to begin now to do all we can to reconnect with and give thanks to our Divine Mother.

Below is a list of some of the things that we can do. You may have many others and I hope you do because what is needed now is a realization that we can and do make a difference to our future, and we can begin with a reorientation of thought and action towards the Earth upon which we live.

- Strive to live up to the positive potential of the planet Earth in your horoscope.
- Always remember Her and realize that She may have been the forgotten planet in our birth chart, but now we can revere and Love Her as we revel in this new found influence and understanding.
- Use the Violet Flame Practice every day of your lives–it will take a few seconds and has tremendous benefit for you and helps us to reconnect to Mother Earth.
- Thank God for Her bounty and thank God for the rain and the drought, the sunshine and the air we breathe.
- Offer our prayers of gratitude each day of our lives—make every day Earth Day.
- Use the beautiful prayers of *The Twelve Blessings*, including The Seventh Blessing: Blessed is The Mother Earth.[11]
- Live and breathe our Love of Mother Earth, knowing that through Her sacrifice, She allows us to live and breathe.
- Raise our own vibrations through service and spiritual action, as the Earth in Her Evolution and through Her

Initiation has risen Her vibrations.

- Understand and appreciate Her kingdom of Nature.
- Learn as much as we can about the Devic Kingdom and cooperate with the nature spirits.
- Travel to Earth's sacred sites—there are many here in the US. Holy mountains charged by ancient Intelligences, such as Mount Adams, Castle Peak, Mount Baldy.[9]
- Learn about the global healing Mission, *Operation Sunbeam*, in which Spiritual energy is sent to Mother Earth. This Mission was devised in 1966 by Dr. George King to make a token karmic repayment to Mother Earth on behalf of humanity—to help balance our debt to Her.[10]
- Always live in a spirit of gratitude for Earth and Her Bounty; and make this the center of our Spiritual life—for without the Earth, we would be lost in Space.
- Always think of Her and pray for Her as the great advanced Spiritual Intelligence that She is, beyond our true comprehension and yet so very close to us.
- Always remember Her Beauty, Her Grace, Her Love, and Her Sacrifice.
- Above all, always remember that we are not only children of God, but also children of Mother Earth. We should always remember that it is Her sacrifice, over millions of years, that enables us to continue our experience.

Earth, Holy Mother

Earth, holy Mother, source of nature,
You feed us while we live, hold us when we die.
Everything comes from you, everything returns to you.
What else could we call you but Our Mother?
Even the Gods call you that.
Without you there is nothing.
Nothing can thrive, nothing can live without your power.
You are all-powerful and my needs are so small.

Give me what I ask. In exchange, I will give you
My thanks, sincere and from my deepest heart.
—Roman Hymn, *Healing Prayers*

We should always remember that the Earth upon which we live is extremely advanced and, like any living intelligence, has feelings and thoughts and is sensitive to the life that exists upon Her body. The Earth is one of the most beautiful planets in this solar system. When the astronauts reached out into space for the first time, the Earth inspired them all and moved many of them to tears. They saw her beauty and her fragility and realized that it is not the Earth that has boundaries—only humanity. However, even more beautiful than Her body, is the indescribable depths of Her compassionate soul. She has dimmed Her light for us; She has sacrificed Her own evolution so that we, ungrateful humanity, can continue our vital journey through experience. She has given us the essence of Her heart; can we give some of our heart, our passion, our love and our gratitude to Her in return?

About Chrissie Blaze

Chrissie Blaze is a London-trained, US-based astrologer whose work spans multiple cultures as a speaker, teacher, author and consultant in astrology, metaphysics and the spiritual sciences. After training at the prestigious Faculty of Astrological Studies in London, she built a private practice with an international clientele. After many years of teaching and lecturing throughout England, she moved her practice to the USA in 1994. As a master consulting astrologer with a multi-layered approach, Blaze's work combines a strong analytical background together with a well-developed intuition and spiritual perspectives. Her interest in working with karmic and past life patterns emerged after working with clients over many years. She is above all a teacher, who believes that astrology is such a practical, helpful tool that it should be available to more people. Her teaching book on astrology *How to Read Your Horoscope in 5 Easy Steps* was first published in 2008. She is also the author of the popular, *Mercury Retrograde*, as well as *Baby Star Signs* (published in several languages), *Superstar Signs* and *Karmic Astrology* as well as several other spiritual and metaphysical books, including the bestselling book, co-authored with Gary Blaze, *Power Prayer*.

**Follow Chrissie Blaze on Facebook and Twitter at
www.Facebook.com/Chrissie.Blaze
and www.Twitter/ChrissieBlaze**

Dear Reader

Thank you very much for your interest in *Earth: Astrology's Missing Planet*. I hope you enjoyed reading the book as much as I enjoyed writing it! If you have a few moments, I would be grateful if you would kindly add your review of *Earth* at your favorite online site. Also, if you would like to see my previous books on astrology and spirituality, please visit my websites at http://www.astrologycity.com and http://www.chrissieblaze.com

Blessings,
Chrissie Blaze

Bibliography

Aivanhov, Omraam Mikhael. *The Living Book of Nature*. Prosveta USA, 1987.

Bailey, Alice. *Esoteric Astrology: Volume III: A Treatise on the Seven Rays*. Lucis Pub., New York, 1951.

Blavatsky, H.P., *The Secret Doctrine: The Synthesis of Science, Religion and Philosophy*. The Theosophical Univ. Press, 1999.

Bohm, David. *Wholeness and the Implicate Order*. Routledge, 2002.

Blaze, Chrissie. *Superstar Signs: Sun Signs of Heroes and You*. Dodona Books, 2008.

Blaze, Chrissie. *Healing Prayers: Blessings from the Heart*. Createspace, 2013.

Clow, Barbara Hand. *Chiron: Rainbow Bridge Between the Inner and Outer Planets*. Llewellyn Publications, 1994.

Einstein, Albert and George Bernard Shaw. *Einstein on Cosmic Religion and Other Opinions and Aphorisms*. Dover Publications, 2009.

Hodson, Geoffrey. *Kingdom of the Gods*. The Theosophical Publishing House, 1970.

Hodson, Geoffrey. *The Brotherhood of Angels and Men*. Ariel Press, 2011.

Hutchison, Michael. *Mega Brain Power: Transform Your Life with Mind Machines and Brain Nutrients*. CreateSpace Independent Publishing Platform, 2013.

Keneipp, Brian C. *Operation Earth Light: A Glimpse into the World of the Ascended Masters*. Aetherius Society, 2000.

King, George. *Spiritual Energy Crisis* audio lecture, Aetherius Press.

King, George. *The Twelve Blessings*, Aetherius Society, 1958.

King, George. *The Nine Freedoms*. Aetherius Society, 1963.

King, George. *Operation Sunbeam: God's Magic in Action*. Kindle edition. The Aetherius Society, 2014.

King, George and Richard Lawrence. *Realize Your Inner Potential – Through the path of spiritual service – King Yoga.* Aetherius Society, 2016.

Lawrence, Richard and Mark Bennett. *Gods, Guides and Guardian Angels,* O-Books, 2007.

Lovelock, James. *Gaia: A New Look at Life on Earth.* Oxford University Press, 2000.

Mitchell, Edgar. *The Way of the Explorer,* New Page Books, 2008.

Endnotes

1 Since trillions of watts of microwaves have been poured into the atmosphere, according to www.earthpulse.net, this is now boosting the average Schumann frequency. Also, the Schumann Resonance encompasses an entire range of frequencies from .01 to well over 100 Hz.

2 "The Cosmic Plan" audio lecture.

3 The Aetherius Society is an international metaphysical organization dedicated to the healing of the individual and the world. www.aetherius.org

4 The Nine Freedoms by Dr. George King. Published by The Aetherius Society.

5 *The Violet Flame Practice published* in Realize *Your Inner Potential – Spiritual Service through King Yoga* by George King and Richard Lawrence, Aetherius Press, 3rd Edition, 2016.

6 In Operation Sunbeam spiritual energy is sent to the Mother Earth, who has sacrificed so much to enable us to live here. The colossal spiritual debt we owe the Earth puts us, as a planetary race, in a grave karmic position, since it is not possible, by Divine Law, to endlessly take without ever giving anything back in return. Operation Sunbeam was devised by Dr. King in 1966 to help solve this problem.

7 For further information on The Violet Flame practice, please refer to *Realize Your Inner Potential – Spiritual Service through King Yoga*

8 *Last Child in the Woods: Saving Our Children from Nature-Deficit Disorder.* But since Richard Louv's book came out in 2005

9 For more information about The Holy Mountains of the World, please visit www.aetherius.org

10 To learn about Operation Sunbeam, please visit www.aetherius.org

11 For more information, please visit www.12blessings.org